# Vintage Knits

# Vintage Knits

25 classic patterns for modern knitters

*from the National Library of Australia*

# Contents

Introduction 6

Revival: knitting in the 21st century 14

**Women 17**

**Judith 18**

Wool in Australia 23

**Patricia 25**

Yarn bombing 28

**Sandra 30**

**Vivian 35**

**Florence 38**

20th-century knitting 42

**Barbara 45**

**Dorothea 48**

Yarn tales 52

**Margaret 54**

Vintage knitting styles and yarns 59

**Helen 60**

Machines take over 64

The world wide knitting web 65

**Men 67**

**Jack 69**

**Clyde 72**

Knitting therapy 76

Ganseys, guernseys and jerseys 77

**Stuart 79**

Sheep breeds and their wool 82
**William** **84**
**Robert** **89**
Breaking records 91

## Children 93

**Lynette** **94**
Knitting for a cause 96
**Pamela** **99**
**Lorraine** **102**
Purling in protest 106
**Beverly** **108**
**Jennifer** **112**
**Fredrick** **116**
Literary knitters 121
**Josephine** **122**
**David** **127**
**Douglas** **130**
A brief history of knitting 136
**Ian** **138**
Knitting guilds 142
**Noni** **144**
Knitting for victory 148

References 152
List of illustrations 154
Acknowledgements 156

# Introduction

## UP TO DATE

Knitting fabric for clothing is a skill that dates back to prehistoric times. Arising as a method of creating fabric from materials such as plant fibres and animal hair, the domestication of sheep yielded woollen yarn that could be knitted as well as woven into warm and comfortable fabrics. Through the Dark Ages and medieval times, knitting as a domestic skill continued (see page 136), right up to the Industrial Revolution when machines took over the mass production of both woven and knitted fabrics (see page 47). Jane Austen mentions genteel ladies 'netting purses' in her novels, while George Eliot has Maggie knitting stockings in *The Mill on the Floss*, showing that knitting for practical purposes was already the main reason for the craft.

By the early years of the twentieth century, knitting had become something that people did as a labour of love; homemakers knitted jumpers and cardigans to keep their families warm. During the World Wars and the Depression years, it was valued as a way of extending the scarce resources of the family and this is reflected in many of the patterns in this book, which mainly come from that era. Tricks to eke out a small budget, or make plain materials look like luxury goods are often referred to in the pages of the women's magazines from which these patterns are taken. The Noni child's cardigan on page 146 was designed to make ordinary wool look like luxury mohair; the Margaret jacket on page 54 was a substitute for an expensive silk blouse.

Knitting was a homely craft, and as women's work moved out of the home it lost its popularity for a generation of women. It has only been in the past few decades that the skill has found a resurgence among younger people who are looking for a creative activity to occupy their leisure hours.

Although the craft has changed in many ways in the past hundred years, the basic skills are the same. If you know how to hold a pair of knitting needles, how to make a knit stitch and a purl stitch, you can knit just about anything.

## HOW TO KNIT

If you've never knitted before—or you learned long ago but have forgotten the basics—the best way to learn is to find a friend or relative who can teach you face to face. If that's not possible, many yarn and craft stores offer lessons for small groups. Another alternative is to use the internet, where many experienced knitters have posted video tutorials showing you how to get started. Just type 'learn to knit' into the search box and follow the links down the rabbit hole until you find a teacher whose style suits you. These video tutorials can also be a good resource if you're an experienced knitter trying a new type of stitch pattern for the first time.

## USING VINTAGE PATTERNS

Vintage knitting patterns like the ones in this book can be a challenge to follow. One of the most common problems is assumed knowledge. In the first half of the twentieth century, the pattern writers and publishers thought that most of their readers would be fairly experienced knitters, so they often didn't bother to define their terms and explain how to achieve certain effects. In this book we've filled in some of the gaps to make the patterns easier to follow for a modern, perhaps not-so-experienced knitter.

## TENSION SQUARE

It's impossible to emphasise enough the importance of knitting a test swatch (some people call it a tension square). This is a piece of knitted fabric using the main yarn and the main needle size of the pattern. It's usually made at least 12cm squared, which is large enough to measure and count stitches. If you've chosen a complicated stitch pattern, it's also a good idea to knit a test swatch in the pattern, to make sure you understand how to do it.

## YARN CHOICE

One of the biggest difficulties in using a vintage pattern is finding a modern yarn that is the equivalent of the original recommended yarn. Very few of the yarns recommended for the patterns in this book are still available and the ways of describing the thickness (or ply) are no longer the same. For example, the Robert pattern on page 89 recommended a fine crochet yarn: we used a modern five-ply and found that we achieved the desired results. See also page 59 for more tips on vintage to modern yarn conversions.

In order to work out what thickness of modern yarn to use, it's better to look at the recommended knitting needle size and tension (stitch count). You will usually find a recommended needle size and stitch count on the label of modern yarns, so use this as a guide. Here's where knitting a test swatch or tension square is important: after you make up a sample measuring at least 12cm squared, wash it and block it (see Finishing the garment, page 10) and lay it flat (without stretching it) on an ironing board or folded towel. Use a ruler or tape measure to measure a 10cm square in the centre of the swatch and mark it with pins. Now you can count the number of stitches between the pins across the row, and compare it with the number of stitches recommended for the pattern. Then count the number of rows between the pins at top and bottom. If the number of stitches (and rows) is the same as recommended, you are all set. If it's not, but it's only a stitch or two different, try adjusting the needle size (see Knitting needle conversions, below).

If the stitch count is very different, you might need to try a different thickness of yarn.

As a general rule of thumb, for modern 100 per cent wool yarns the following stitch counts apply:

**4 ply (fingering) yarn**
3.25mm needles
28 stitches and 36 rows to 10cm square

**8 ply (double knitting or DK) yarn**
4.0mm needles
22 stitches and 28 rows to 10cm square

**12 ply (heavyweight) yarn**
5.5mm needles
16 stitches and 22 rows to 10cm square

Try to select yarn of similar composition to the original; that is, if the pattern recommends 100 per cent wool, choose a modern 100 per cent wool yarn. Most of the patterns in this book use only natural-fibre yarns such as wool, mohair and angora, as acrylic yarns were not invented until the 1940s and were not manufactured in commercial amounts until the 1950s. If you want to knit with acrylics or other modern yarns such as sustainable bamboo, be aware that, even if your test swatch is correct, the different qualities of the yarn could mean that the garment may not drape or stretch the same way as the original.

## COLOUR CHOICE

Modern yarns, thanks to innovations in dyeing technology, are available in a much wider range of clear, bright colours than in the past. This is one of the delights of knitting your own garments: you get to choose exactly which colour you would like to wear.

## NEEDLE SIZES

In the early twentieth century, knitting needles were numbered by their gauge or diameter (thickness), measured as if it were wire. The number indicates how many diameters fit across an inch, so the larger the number, the thinner the needle. For example, a 4.0mm needle is a size 8, meaning that eight needles laid next to each other would be an inch across; a 2.75mm needle is a size 12, meaning that you would need twelve needles laid parallel to make an inch.

These days, most needle diameters are measured and numbered in millimetres, which makes it easier. The exception to both of these numbering systems is in America, where the numbers go from 0 (thin) to 15 (thick) and don't reflect any measurements. The table below will help you work out what size needle you need to use. It's also worth investing in a needle gauge (usually a flat piece of plastic with various sized holes in it that you pass the needle through) to ensure the correct needle size.

**Knitting needle conversions**

| Diameter in mm | Gauge | (US size) |
|---|---|---|
| 2.0 | 14 | (0) |
| 2.25 | 13 | (1) |
| 2.75 | 12 | (2) |
| 3.0 | 11 | (--) |
| 3.25 | 10 | (3) |
| 3.75 | 9 | (5)* |
| 4.0 | 8 | (6) |
| 4.5 | 7 | (7) |
| 5.0 | 6 | (8) |
| 5.5 | 5 | (9) |
| 6.0 | 4 | (10) |
| 6.5 | 3 | (10½) |
| 7.0 | 2 | (--) |
| 7.5 | 1 | (--) |
| 8.0 | 0 | (11) |
| 9.0 | 00 | (13) |
| 10.0 | 000 | (15) |

*US no. 4 needles are 3.5mm

Once you've worked out what size needle is recommended, knit a test swatch to check that it gives the desired number of stitches. If you are a tight knitter and you have too many stitches, try using needles one size larger. If you are a loose knitter and have too few stitches, try using needles one size smaller than recommended.

**Crochet hook conversions**

| Diameter in mm | Old size | (US) |
|---|---|---|
| 2.0 | 14 | (B/1) |
| 2.5 | 12 | (C/2) |
| 3.0 | 11 | (--) |
| 3.25 | 10 | (D/3) |
| 3.5 | 9 | (E/4) |
| 4.0 | 8 | (G/6) |
| 4.5 | 7 | (7) |
| 5.0 | 6 | (H/8) |
| 5.5 | 5 | (I/5) |
| 6.0 | 4 | (J/10) |
| 6.5 | 3 | (K/10.5) |
| 7.0 | 2 | (--) |
| 8.0 | 0 | (--) |

## MEASURING UP

Many vintage patterns were not designed in the range of sizes that are usually given in modern knitting patterns, and people in general are taller and wider than the average male or female (both adults and children) of many years ago. Check your body measurements carefully against those given in the pattern, and don't forget to knit a test swatch to check the stitch count.

If you want to change the size of the garment from that given in the pattern, here are some simple tips on how to do it.

To go up one size (about 5cm larger), use needles one size larger than recommended. Make sure you knit a test swatch with the larger needles and count the stitches, then you can work out the finished dimensions to check that the new size will be correct. To do this, count the number of stitches over 10cm in your larger test swatch. Divide the desired measurement of the garment by 10. Multiply by the number of stitches in the swatch to check that the new number is close to the number of stitches in the pattern. Don't forget to check the row count: some patterns tell you to knit a certain number of rows rather than a length in centimetres.

To go down one size (about 5cm smaller), use needles one size smaller than recommended and check the measurements against your test swatch as above.

If you want to increase (or decrease) by two sizes (10cm) or more, it's better to add stitches (and rows) where you need them. This is easier if it's a plain knit fabric or the pattern has a small repeat (such as a rib stitch, which usually repeats after only two or four stitches), but if it's a lacy or complicated pattern, you might not want to attempt adding stitches unless you are a confident knitter. Make sure that you increase in multiples of the pattern repeat if there is one. To work out how many stitches to add, knit a test swatch to check the stitch count. If you want to add 20cm to the chest measurement of the garment, you'll need to add 10cm each to the front and back, so add the number of stitches you counted in your test swatch. Don't forget to consider the additional stitches when it comes time to cast off for armholes or necklines. It may be helpful to draw out the tricky parts of the pattern (such as armholes and necklines) on graph paper so you can work out how to shape them with the additional stitches. Remember that you will also need to increase (or decrease) the width and length of the sleeves.

If a larger garment is required, add 12mm on both the back and front armhole shaping to the shoulder. For a smaller garment, reduce the length of the armhole shaping to the shoulder by 12mm.

When converting from imperial (inches) measurements in the original patterns to metric (centimetres) we used the following approximate conversions:

| Inches | Centimetres |
|---|---|
| 1 | 2.5 |
| 2 | 5 |
| 3 | 7.5 |
| 4 | 10 |
| 5 | 13 |
| 6 | 15 |
| 7 | 18 |
| 8 | 20 |
| 9 | 23 |
| 10 | 25.5 |
| 11 | 28 |
| 12 | 30.5 |
| 14 | 36 |
| 16 | 40.5 |
| 18 | 46 |
| 20 | 51 |
| 22 | 56 |
| 24 | 61 |
| 16 | 66 |
| 28 | 71 |
| 30 | 76 |
| 32 | 81 |
| 34 | 86 |
| 36 | 92 |
| 38 | 96.5 |
| 40 | 102 |

## FINISHING THE GARMENT

When all of the pieces of the garment are knitted, you'll need to sew them together. Use the same yarn that you used to knit the fabric, and thread it into a wool needle with a large eye and a blunt point. Some knitters like to use ladder or mattress stitch, which is worked with the pieces laid flat, right side up. Others prefer a backstitch seam, sewn with the right sides of the knitted fabric together. Still others like to use a crochet hook to join two pieces of knitting.

After the garment is assembled the final step is to block it. To do this, lay a thick towel or cloth on a flat surface. Dampen the garment by spraying it with cool water or handwashing it. Spread it out on the towel, gently pulling it into shape as you do so. Leave it to dry flat in the shade. Some of the patterns in this book recommend using an iron on the wool setting and a cloth to press the garment from the wrong side.

## GARMENT CARE

Modern yarns will often be labelled machine washable, making cleaning much easier. Wool and other natural fibres, such as silk, mohair and alpaca, that are not labelled machine washable can be handwashed in lukewarm or cool water, using a gentle soap or detergent. There are specialty woolwash soaps and detergents available, some of which don't even need to be rinsed out of the garment as they provide a protective layer to the yarn.

Do not wring out a knitted garment or peg it on a clothesline to dry. Instead, press as much water as you can out of the fabric using your hands and then lay it on a thick towel. Roll it up in the towel and squeeze: the towel will absorb a lot of the water. Lastly, lay it flat on a dry towel or blocking mat and gently pull it into shape without stretching it. Leave it to dry flat, out of direct sunlight.

## ABBREVIATIONS AND TERMS

In this book we have used the following common abbreviations and terms:

**k** knit (sometimes called 'plain')

**p** purl

**sl** slip

**alt** alternate

**beg** beginning

**DC** double crochet

**dec** decrease (subtract a stitch): in these patterns, this is usually achieved by knitting (or purling) two stitches together. There are many ways that people like to do this, so feel free to choose whichever method serves you best.

**DPNs** double-pointed needles

**garter stitch** knit all stitches in every row

**inc** increase (add a stitch): the method often used in these patterns is to knit twice into the same stitch. Modern patterns tend to say KFB (knit into front and back of the stitch). There are other ways to increase, so again you should feel free to use the method that serves you best.

**moss stitch** k 1, p1 across the row, then on the wrong side of the work, knit into the right-side knit stitches and purl into the purl stitches so that the stitches in each row alternate directions. You can also knit a k 2, p 2 moss stitch.

**psso** pass slipped stitch over the last stitch knitted

**rep** repeat

**rib** a combination of knit and purl stitches knitted in columns; for example, k 1, p 1 or k 2, p 2. Rarely, it can be other combinations, such as k 3, p 1 with the wrong-side rows being k 1, p 3.

**ssk** slip, slip, knit (slip next two stitches knitwise, one at a time, to right-hand needle, return stitches to the left-hand needle facing the other way and k 2 tog (this makes a left-leaning decrease).

**stocking stitch** knit all stitches in the right-side rows and purl all stitches in the wrong-side rows

**tbl** through back of loop

**tog** together (as in k 2 tog)

**yrn** yarn round needle. Bring the yarn around the needle before knitting or purling the next stitch; some patterns refer to this as yarn (or wool) forward.

## HINTS TO KNITTERS

*from The Australian Women's Weekly Homemaker Section, 13 April 1935.*

- Where the work has increasings and decreasings it is a good plan to tie a piece of coloured thread where these come, as otherwise it is difficult to keep them regular and any irregularity spoils the appearance of the work.
- Be very careful about the neckline and armholes. Usually the stitches are carefully 'picked up' and the edge or border knitted on finer needles. A crochet edge is firm and makes an attractive finish to a jumper with a V-neck and also to sleeveless armholes.
- **Never** join on a fresh ball of wool except at the beginning of a row and darn in all the ends very carefully on the wrong side.

## A NOTE ON PATTERN NAMES

The original editors liked to give knitting patterns 'human' names, such as Florence, Clive or Noni. For consistency, we've named all of the patterns in this book the same way. If they didn't have a personal name in the original source, we chose one from a list of the most popular baby names of the 1940s in Australia.

DAPHNE
CROCHET WOOL
SHADE
X331
Just the
pullover
bands w
MATERIALS REQU
Two skeins Linc
3-ply wool; 1 pair
pair No. 12 needles
MEASUREMENTS:
Length from top of
underarm, 12"; widt
22".
For abbreviations

“Fredrick”
WHEN BREEZES BLOW
for those cooler summer days is this neat
intriguing new stitch. With the neck
it is very quickly knitted.
“Daphne”
needles and 1
FRONT.—
sts., and
No. 12
rib
row
10
row
16”; length
P 2, k 2
st.), p 2, k 2 (knit
1, k 4,

# Revival: knitting in the 21st century

This ancient craft was once a staple of a woman's education, but the twentieth century saw its decline as mass production took the creation of garments out of the home and into the chain stores. Recent years have seen a resurgence of interest, and not only among women.

A knitter taking part in a yarn bombing event at Central Park Mall in Sydney in 2016.

During the mid-twentieth century, following years of knitting for the war effort and to save money during the straitened times of the Great Depression, knitting continued to be practised as a domestic skill in the 1950s and 1960s, with the introduction of new colours, synthetic yarns and patterns giving it a modern kick. However, the feminist movement of the 1960s enabled many women to engage in activities other than homemaking tasks, and as women entered the workforce outside the home they had less time and more disposable income, so they preferred to purchase ready-made clothing. Low-cost machine-knitted items were mass-produced, and easy-care synthetic fibres had become popular. By the 1980s, interest in handknitting had waned and the skill was beginning to be lost.

The years around the turn of the twenty-first century saw a resurgence of interest in knitting. Natural fibres were once again widely available and luxury fibres that had been scarce for most of the twentieth century were cheaper; for example, alpaca, angora and merino, as well as cotton, silk and—a new and sustainable natural fibre—bamboo. Time-poor people began to understand the value of unique handknitted garments as a luxury and wanted to learn how to make them.

As a sign of the rise in popularity, the first worldwide Knit in Public Day was held in 2005, and is still celebrated in June each year.

The 'handmade revolution' coincided with the widespread adoption of social media platforms such as Facebook and Instagram, which enabled people to share information around the globe.

Knitters attend a workshop in Sydney's Redfern in 2016.

In 2007, an international social networking site, Ravelry.com, began helping knitters to manage their projects and share patterns and ideas. By the end of 2020, Ravelry.com had more than nine million registered users.

People enjoy knitting for a range of reasons. It provides a creative outlet and sense of accomplishment. Knitters report that the craft helps them cope with stress and feel productive, and some have even used it as a means to give up smoking. It enables people to multitask—a valuable skill in the modern world—since knitting can be done alongside other activities, such as commuting, watching television or listening to a podcast. People have even been seen knitting at sporting events and in theatres. The process of yarn around needle provides a calming effect for fidgety people, and those who belong to a social knitting group use the opportunity to make friends with other knitters.

Celebrities who knit, such as Nicole Kidman, Audrey Hepburn, the Duchess of Cambridge, Lorde, Meryl Streep, Patrick Stewart and Julia Roberts have helped to make knitting more popular. British diver Tom Daley won many hearts and minds during the 2021 Olympics when he was spotted watching the competition from the stands while working on his knitting. He even made a tiny little sweater for his gold medal!

Whether you knit to indulge your creative side or just to keep yourself from fidgeting, it's a craft with appeal to many. One of the best things about it is that you can wear your unique creation proudly when you're finished.

# Women

Women's magazines and knitting patterns of the mid-twentieth century tended to focus on practicality and frugality as well as style. Knitting in those times was still very much the domain of the housewife, although girls and young women were expected to take up the needles from a young age.

One of the interesting features of the knitting patterns for women at this time is the fact that they were not as size-inclusive as they are today. This is partly because homemakers were expected to be skilled knitters who knew how to make the adjustments required to make a garment in the size desired. It also reflects in some ways that women's magazine and other publications focussed on the ideal: the ideal home, the ideal housewife, the ideal face and the ideal figure.

A slim yet curvy figure and elegant outfits were promoted as the desire of every woman. The descriptions of these patterns include words like 'slender', 'youthful' and 'smart'. Figure-hugging knits with cute little collars and short sleeves emphasised femininity and girlishness.

Adding these timeless knitted garments to your modern wardrobe is sure to make you stand out from the crowd.

# Judith

For chic simplicity you will find this alluring little jumper hard to beat.

*The Australian Women's Weekly*, 27 February, 1937.

**Materials:** 400g Patons Bluebell Merino 5 ply. 1 pair each of 3.00mm and 3.75mm needles (a tight knitter may have to substitute 4.00mm needles for the latter to get the right tension). 10 buttons. Stitch holders.

**Measurements:** Bust 86–92cm (the rib being fairly stretchy); length 46cm; sleeve seam 12cm. This garment has negative ease, which means it is designed to cling to the curves of the body.

**Tension:** 34 stitches to 10cm, measured over the fancy ribbing lightly patted flat.

**Pattern stitch:** Twist 2. To twist 2, take needle round the back of next stitch, and bringing point to the front between the next 2 stitches, knit the second, then knit the first and drop both loops off left-hand needle together.

## BACK

With 3.00mm needles, cast on 126 stitches. Knit first row into backs of stitches, then work in k 1, p 1, rib for 7cm. Changing to 3.75mm needles, proceed as follows:

**1st row:** Sl 1, * k 2, p 1, k 1, p 1, repeat from * to end.

**2nd row:** * K 1, p 1, k 1, p 2, repeat from * to last stitch, k 1.

**3rd row:** Sl 1, * twist 2, p 1, k 1, p 1, repeat from * to end.

The last 2 rows form the pattern, repeated throughout. Continuing in pattern thus, increase at each end of every 8th row (taking new stitches into pattern as they appear) till there are 144 stitches on needle. Work should now measure about 30cm from cast on. If necessary, do a few more rows to achieve the length you desire.

Enchantingly fresh-looking, this jumper has a naïve round neckline. The original used Pagoda Crepe, a wool yarn with silk in the twist. We've updated it with a 100% merino wool crepe-style yarn. The twisted rib stitch is actually quite simple to knit.

Shape armholes by casting off 7 stitches at beg of next 2 rows and then decreasing 1 stitch at each end of following 5 rows (120 stitches). Continue straight till back measures 40cm from cast-on edge, ending with a wrong side row. Here, shape for yoke as follows:

**1st row:** Work 46 stitches in pattern; turn, and work back in pattern. (Work the 2nd and all even rows in pattern.)

**3rd row:** Work 43 stitches in pattern; turn, and work back in pattern.

**5th row:** Work 40 stitches in pattern; turn, and work back in pattern.

**7th row:** Work 36 stitches in pattern; turn, and work back in pattern.

**9th row:** Work 33 stitches in pattern; turn, and work back in pattern.

**11th row:** Work 30 stitches in pattern; turn, and work back in pattern.

**13th row:** Work 26 stitches in pattern; turn, and work back in pattern.

**15th row:** Work 23 stitches in pattern; turn, and work back in pattern.

**17th row:** Work 20 stitches in pattern; turn, and work back in pattern.

**19th row:** Work 18 stitches in pattern; turn, and work back in pattern.

**21st row:** Knit 18 stitches in pattern, without twisting the rib, then place these 18 stitches on a stitch holder. Place next 56 stitches on another stitch holder.

Join wool at neck edge of remaining 46 stitches, and work in pattern to end. Now work as given for opposite shoulder, from 1st to 19th and 20th rows inclusive. Knit 18 stitches and place them on a stitch holder. Place remaining stitches on another stitch holder. Leave all these stitches for the present.

## FRONT

With 3.00mm needles, cast on 126 stitches. Knit first row into the backs of cast-on stitches, then work in k 1, p 1 ribbing to match back welt. Changing to 3.75mm needles, proceed as follows:

6 The AUSTRALIAN WOMEN'S WEEKLY Saturday, February 27, 1937.

MARCH OF THE MODE by Rene

NEWER KNITWEAR

*Full directions for making these smart knitted models are given in the accompanying free knitting supplement.*

● At Left: "Judith": Directions for making appear on page 6 of supplement.

● Above: "SHERLEY": Directions for making appear on page 4 of supplement.

● Above: "ELEANOR": Directions for making appear on page 8 of supplement.

● At left: "ELIZABETH": Directions for making appear on page 5 of supplement.

**Left front:**

**1st row:** Sl 1, * k 2, p 1, k 1, p 1, repeat from * 10 times more, k 2, turn, leaving remaining 68 stitches on spare needle or stitch holder.

**2nd row:** Cast on 10 stitches to create buttonhole band. Knit into backs of cast-on stitches, * p 2, k 1, p 1, k 1, repeat from * to last 3 stitches, p 2, k 1.

**3rd row:** Sl 1, * twist 2, p 1, k 1, p 1, repeat from * to last 12 stitches, twist 2, (p 1, k 1) five times.

**4th row:** Sl first stitch purlwise, k 1, (p 1, k 1) four times, * p 2, k 1, p 1, k 1, repeat from * to last 3 stitches, p 2, k 1.

Continuing thus in pattern with a ribbed

buttonhole band, increase at side seam edge in 8th, and every following 8th row till there are 77 stitches on the needle.

When side seam edge matches that of back, shape armhole by casting off 7 stitches at that edge, working to end and back, and then decreasing at armhole end of next 5 rows (60 stitches).

Carry on straight after armhole shaping is completed till work measures 40cm from commencement, ending at armhole edge.

Shape for yoke exactly as given for first shoulder of back (1st to 20th rows inclusive). Cast off 18 stitches. Place remaining stitches onto a stitch holder.

Before working right front, mark positions of 9 of the buttons on left front with pins, the top one just about 2 rows below the top of the part so far completed, and eight more at equal intervals of about 4cm. This should bring the bottom one to a position about 2cm above the welt. (The tenth buttonhole is worked as part of the collar shaping.)

**Right front:**

Now join wool to centre-front edge of the remaining 68 stitches.

**1st row:** (K 1, p 1) five times, * k 2, p 1, k 1, p 1, repeat from * to last 3 stitches, k 3.

**2nd row:** Sl 1, * p 2, k 1, p 1, k 1, repeat from * to last 12 stitches, p 2 (k 1, p 1) four times, k 2.

**3rd row:** (K 1, p 1) five times, * twist 2, p 1, k 1, p 1, repeat from * to last 3 stitches, twist 2, k 1.

Continuing thus in pattern, increase at side seam edge in every 8th row as for left front, and also make buttonholes (as follows; see page 22) in the ribbed buttonhole band to match positions marked for buttons on left front.

**Buttonholes:**
To make a buttonhole, cast off the 5th and 6th stitches from the edge of the border, and cast them on again in the next row.
Finish the right front to correspond with left front (with nine buttonholes in all).

## COLLAR

Now join the shoulder seams neatly, using a three-needle cast off. With the wrong side of the work facing, pick up on a 3.00mm needle all the stitches left at the top of left front, back and right front. From here the yoke is worked entirely in k 1, p 1, rib starting on 3.00mm needles. In the first row, pick up extra stitches where gaps occur (this will be necessary over the shoulders). You should have 193 stitches finally, which allows for picking up an extra 15 stitches thus. Take care to keep the continuity of rib in the bands at the front.
Work 4cm in k 1, p 1 rib, ending at buttonhole edge. Make a buttonhole above the others in the next two rows.
**Next row:** Cast off 10 stitches in rib, rib to end.
**Next row:** Cast off 10 stitches in rib, * p 12, p 2 tog, p 2 tog, repeat from * to last 13 stitches, p 13 (this purl row makes a ridge as the wrong side to mark the 'turn-over' of collar). Work eight more rows in rib. Change to 3.75mm needles and work another eight rows of rib, as loosely as possible (if you have a pair of 4.00mm needles by you, use those to cast off loosely).

## SLEEVES

With 3.00mm needles, cast on 86 stitches. Work 16 rows in k 1, p 1 rib. Change to 3.75mm needles and pattern, and continue straight for 5cm. Increase at each end of next and every alternate row till there are 92 stitches. Pattern part of sleeve should now measure about 7.5cm. If necessary, work another two or three rows straight.
**Shape top of sleeve:**
Cast off 3 stitches at beginning of next 2 rows. 86 stitches.
Decrease 1 stitch at each end of every row eight times. 70 stitches.
Decrease 1 stitch at each end of every right side row four times. 62 stitches.
Decrease 1 stitch at each end of every row eight times. 46 stitches.
Cast off 3 stitches at beginning of next two rows. 40 stitches remain. Cast off.

## MAKING UP

Press pieces very lightly under a damp cloth (but not the k 1, p 1 rib at all). Sew the sleeves in flat, then join side and sleeve seams. You may wish to turn down the collar and work a row of double crochet along the fold to give a good sharp turning. Sew on buttons to correspond with buttonholes. Turn back the cuffs and catch into position.

# Wool in Australia

The story of wool production in Australia is a tale of survival and necessity at one end, and success and high fashion at the other. In the early years of the colony of New South Wales, chaplain and farmer Samuel Marsden selectively bred sheep, crossing Merinos with Southdowns and Suffolks, robust British short-wool breeds that produced good meat. Pressures of the new settlement meant that sheep were needed for both fleece and food.

In 1801, the first woollen mill in Australia was built at Parramatta, 23 kilometres west of Sydney Cove. Using female convict labour supervised by Marsden, this mill produced blanketing from the fleeces of 400 local sheep, a sign of the young colony's priorities and limited capabilities. The British Government's directive was that their New South Wales colony was to produce only the rougher types of cloth, reserving the best wool for export back to England where finer textiles would be woven.

Wool growing soon produced rewards. Visiting England in 1807, Marsden wore a suit made from his own sheep's wool when he met King George III, who was so captivated that Marsden had one made for him from the same material. The King's reward to Marsden was a present of Merinos from his own stud.

By 1814, the Parramatta mill had produced its first pair of stockings, made from famously fine Spanish wool. Four years later, Australian fine wool was judged superior to English wool and the demand for it in England grew. Pastoralist and entrepreneur John Macarthur's wool-growing efforts paid off when he won two gold medals in 1822 for producing wool equal in quality to the legendary Saxon or German, famed for the fineness and brilliance of its fleece. The sheep industry continued to expand, with breeders always keen to improve their flocks. By the end of the 1830s there were sheep in every colony.

Perhaps as a sign of increasing confidence, a fabric made at the Parramatta factory in 1838 was called 'Parramatta Tweed'. Tweed is a coarse medium- to heavy-weight material made from wool or wool blends. In the mid-nineteenth century, it was popularised by the Prince of Wales and became the preferred apparel for outdoor pursuits. By the 1870s, the desirability of tweed created even more demand for Australian wool in the English market.

The Peppin brothers, who had migrated from Somerset, England, had begun experimenting with Spanish and French breeds in 1861. At Deniliquin in New South Wales, they produced the Peppin Merino. This breed thrived in a wide range of habitats from subtropical Queensland to cool temperate Tasmania. Clearly superior, it became the most important sheep strain in Australia.

By 1886, three-quarters of New South Wales Merinos were producing combing wool for the growing worsted industry. By the late nineteenth century, wool had become Australia's main export. Australia led the world in wool production, largely responsible for preventing the global textile industry from being taken over by cotton.

The original yarn recommended for this fitted jumper was Nursery Viyella 3 ply. We've updated it with Malabrigo Sock yarn in 'Ravelry Red' (100% Superwash merino wool).

# Patricia

More than a good sports jumper—it's an incentive to go out and play just for the fun of wearing it, and it fits so snugly.

*The Australian Women's Weekly*, 25 March 1939.

**Materials:** 300g Malabrigo Sock 100% wool yarn (approximately 4 ply). 1 pair 3.25mm needles. 2 spare needles or stitch holders.
**Measurements:** Length from shoulder, 47cm. Bust to fit 86–92cm. Sleeve seam, 14cm underarm.
**Tension:** 30 stitches and 52 rows to 10cm.

## BACK

Cast on 97 stitches. K, working into back of stitches on this row only. Work in pattern as follows:
**1st row:** (back of work): K 1, * wool forward, sl 1, k 1 *. Repeat from * to *.
**2nd row:** * K 1, k 2 tog into back of next 2 stitches (the slipped stitch and wool forward stitch of previous row) *. Repeat from * until last stitch, k 1.
These 2 rows form pattern and are repeated throughout garment.
Continue in pattern for 46 rows, then increase 1 stitch at each end of row in next row and every 6th row following until you have 129 stitches. Continue in pattern until work measures 30cm from casting on.
**Shape armholes:** Cast off 8 stitches at beginning of next 2 rows. Then decrease 1 stitch at both ends of next row. Continue decreasing 1 stitch at both ends of alternate rows until 99 stitches remain. Continue on these stitches until work measures 36cm from casting on, ending on a wrong side row.
**Shape for yoke:** Work 26 stitches in pattern. Place remaining 73 stitches on spare needle and continue on these 26 stitches for right back.
**Right side of back:** Cast off 2 stitches at beginning of row, work remaining stitches in pattern, turn, work next row in pattern without shaping. Repeat these 2 rows until all stitches are cast off.

When casting off, work into back of slipped stitch and wool forward stitch and k 2 tog as usual, counting this as 1 stitch. Join wool to stitches on spare needle, cast off 47 stitches, then continue on remaining 26 stitches.
Work **left side of back** to match right side, from * to end.

## FRONT

Work exactly as back.

## YOKE

Cast on 24 stitches. Work in pattern. Increase 1 stitch at both ends of alternate rows until 66 stitches, ending on wrong side of work. Continue on these stitches as follows: Work 23 stitches in pattern, p 20 stitches, work 23 stitches in pattern.
Repeat this row 5 times more.
**Next row:** Work 23 stitches in pattern, p 4, cast off 12 stitches, p 4. Work remaining stitches in pattern. Continue to work on these stitches for front half of yoke, * work 23 stitches in pattern, p 4 (place remaining stitches on spare needle for present).
**Next row:** P 4, work 23 stitches in pattern. Repeat these 2 rows until 58 rows have been worked*, place these stitches on spare needle. Join wool to stitches on first spare needle and work back half of yoke to match, beginning with p 4, work 23 stitches in pattern, then as from * to * of front half.
**Next row:** Work 23 stitches in pattern, p 4, cast on 12 stitches, work across stitches on spare needle, then continue on 66 stitches for 5 more rows, purling the centre 20 stitches as before on every row.
Now work all stitches in pattern. Shape this end of yoke by decreasing 1 stitch at both ends of alternate rows until 24 stitches remain. Cast off.

## SLEEVES (BOTH ALIKE)

Cast on 75 stitches. Work in pattern for 2.5cm, then increase 1 stitch at both ends of next row and every 8th row following until you have 87 stitches. Continue until seam measures 14cm or length required, ending on wrong side of work.
**Shape top:** Cast off 2 stitches at beginning of every row until 23 stitches remain. Cast off.

## MAKING UP

Sew yoke on to matching parts of back and front. Join side seams. Join sleeve seams and insert into armholes. Press all seams with a warm iron over a damp cloth.

# Yarn bombing

Yarn bombing (also known as guerrilla knitting) is a form of street art or graffiti in which public objects are covered with colourful knitted or crocheted creations. Yarn bombing serves a number of purposes: beautifying sterile and unwelcoming public spaces, making art accessible to the general public, encouraging people to participate in street art, bringing communities together, highlighting a cause or making a political statement.

Fabric designer Magda Sayeg is believed to have started the yarn-bombing craze in 2005, when she brightened up her steel-and-concrete surroundings in Houston, Texas, by knitting a doorknob cosy for her shop, followed by a sleeve for the pole of a stop sign. People started getting out of their cars to take photos, and Madga began installing knitted creations everywhere she went.

Yarn bombing can be anything from a small project such as a tree cosy, a post warmer, a scarf on a statue or a pothole filler, to a major installation such as a cover for a car, submarine or bridge. A blanket of pink squares was made to cover an army tank in protest against Denmark's involvement in Iraq. In Australia, Knitting Nannas Against Gas knitted yellow and black triangle flags to protest against mining of coal seam gas.

In the early days, yarn bombers tended to work without permission from local authorities or property owners, often under cover of darkness and using pseudonyms. Magda Sayeg (alias PolyCotN) and her friend A Krylik, created a yarn-bombing crew called Knitta Please. Knitters around the world followed her lead and yarn bombing quickly spread throughout North America, Europe, Scandinavia, Asia and Australasia. The first International Yarn Bombing Day was held on 11 June 2011, and officially sanctioned projects are now commonplace.

In 2015, many groups made yarn poppies for installations to mark the 100th anniversary of the Anzac landings at Gallipoli. Adelaide businesses, charities, councils and artists have worked together on projects, such as *The Knitted City* installations in 2011 and the Victoria Square Christmas celebrations commissioned by the Adelaide City Council in 2012.

In 2014, the town of Holbrook in New South Wales covered their famous submarine landmark in yellow knitted squares to celebrate 50 years since the Beatles toured Australia. Initiated by Murray Arts, the project aimed to attract visitors back to the town after it was bypassed by the Hume Highway.

Since 2013, trees in the National Arboretum Canberra have been dressed in winter with blankets and scarves. *Warm Trees* is thought to be the largest installation of knitting and crochet on trees in the world. At the end of winter, the former tree-warmers are turned into blankets and donated to charity.

Social media has played a powerful role in the spread and popularity of yarn bombing across the world, through sharing photos, instructions, designs and projects, as well as calls for knitters for installations. Have you seen any yarn bombing projects in your neighbourhood? Maybe you would like to start one.

TOP Jane Balke Andersen yarn bombing a tree in Ward Park, Redfern, Sydney; BOTTOM Jane was one of the team behind The Popping Pom Poms installation that covered the park in knitted garments for the 2016 Surry Hills Festival.

# Sandra

An easy-to-make sweater-cum-cardigan that you will adore for its cosiness and air of casual chic—and it's rated for instant success with young things who want something just a bit 'different'. It is so versatile too—and you can wear it to town with a tailored skirt, or for sports with your slacks and shorts.

*The Australian Women's Weekly*, 16 August 1941.

**Materials:** 800g Fiddlesticks Grange Fourteen (40% wool, 40% acrylic, 20% alpaca). 1 pair each of 6.5mm and 7.00mm knitting needles. 4.5mm crochet hook. 8 buttons.
**Measurements:** Length from top of shoulder, 46cm; width all round at underarm, 81cm; length of sleeve from underarm, 15cm.
**Tension:** 12 stitches to 10cm.

## BACK

Using 7.00mm needles, cast on 44 stitches. (With this wool, use thumb method for casting on.)
**1st row:** Sl 1, * yarn forward, sl 1 purlways, k 1, repeat from * to last stitch, p 1.
**2nd row:** Sl 1, * yarn forward, sl 1 purlways, k tog next stitch and the yarn forward loop of previous row, repeat from * to last stitch, p 1.
Repeat 2nd row 8 times.
Increase at beginning and end of next and every following 8th row 4 times (54 stitches).
Continue in pattern until work measures 25cm from casting on.
**Armhole shaping:** Cast off 4 stitches at beginning of next 2 rows, then k 2 tog each end of every alternate row 4 times (36 stitches).
Continue without shaping until work measures 40cm from casting on.
**Shoulder shaping:**
**1st and 2nd rows:** Work in pattern to last 4 stitches, turn.
**3rd and 4th rows:** Work in pattern to last 8 stitches, turn.
**5th and 6th rows:** Work in pattern to end.
Cast off.

## RIGHT FRONT

Cast on 26 stitches. Work in pattern as given for the back. Increase at seam edge as for the back until there are 31sts on needle. Continue until work measures same as back to armholes.

The original pattern used P. & B. Blanket wool. Our suggested modern equivalent is a 14 ply or bulky yarn, but check your tension carefully and go up or down a needle size if necessary. Our knitter found that joining the seams using single crochet gave a neater finish with this bulky wool.

**Armhole shaping:** Cast off 4 stitches at seam edge. Then k 2 tog every alternate row 4 times (22 stitches). Continue in pattern for 12 rows. Shape neck by casting off 4 stitches. Knit to end of row.

Work yoke as follows:

**1st row:** Sl 1, * p into 2nd stitch (do not slip off needle), p into first stitch, slip both stitches off needle. Repeat from * to last stitch, p 1.

**2nd row:** Sl 1, k 2 tog, * k into back of 2nd stitch (do not slip off needle), k into front of first stitch, slip both stitches off needle. Repeat from * to last stitch, p 1. Repeat 1st and 2nd rows once (16 stitches), then continue without shaping until work measures same as back, ending at the neck edge.

**Shoulder shaping:**

**1st row:** Work in pattern to last 5 stitches, turn.

**2nd row:** Work in pattern to end of row.

**3rd row:** Work in pattern to last 11 stitches, turn.

**4th row:** Like second row. Cast off.

## LEFT FRONT

Work as given for the right front to neck. Cast off 4 stitches at front edge. Purl to end of row. Commence pattern on 2nd row of yoke pattern and work to correspond with right front.

## SLEEVES (BOTH ALIKE)

Cast on 34 stitches. Work as given for the back. Increase at beginning and end of 5th and every following 6th row until there are 42 stitches on needle. Work without shaping until work measures 13cm from casting on. K 2 tog each end of next and every alternate row until 20 stitches remain. Cast off 6 stitches at beginning and end of next two rows (8 stitches remain). Work 6 rows in pattern. Cast off.

## CUFFS AND WAISTBAND

**Cuffs:** Using 6.5mm needles, cast on 8 stitches. Knit into back of cast-on stitches.

**1st row:** Sl 1, * with yarn in front, purl into 2nd stitch on the left-hand needle (do not slip off needle). Purl into 1st stitch, slip both stitches off needle. Repeat from * to last stitch, p 1.

**2nd row:** Sl 1, * k into back of 2nd stitch on the left-hand needle (do not slip off needle), k into front of first stitch, slip both stitches off the needle. Repeat from * to last stitch, p 1. Repeat these two rows 16–20 times (to make desired length of cuff). Repeat to make a second cuff.

**Waistband:** Using 6.5mm needles, cast on 18 stitches and work as given for the cuffs, until work measures 66cm (slightly stretched).

## TO MAKE UP

Sew up side and shoulder seams. Join the 6 cast-off stitches of sleeve to knitted edge. Sew up all seams. Sew in sleeves, placing seam to seam. Gather extra fabric at the top of each sleeve to create a puffy effect. Attach cuffs and waistband. With wrong side facing you, commence crochet at waistband of left front. Double crochet along left front, around neck and along right front. Break off wool, commence at left front and work round to right front. Make 8 buttonholes as follows: 1 DC (2 chain, miss 1 DC, 5 DC). Work 1 row more of DC around fronts and neck, if desired. With a damp cloth and warm iron, lightly press all seams. Sew on buttons.

'Ramada' Super Fingering wool in 4 ply was the original requirement for this jumper, but we used Patons Bluebell Merino 100% Merino Wool, a 5 ply yarn. Our sample is sized up to fit a 102cm bust by adding 26 stitches across the front and back. These instructions have been added to the pattern in *italics*.

The pattern on these pages is for the Vivian ribbed jumper in green; instructions for the short-sleeved cardigan (Sandra) can be found on pages 30–33.

# Vivian

Guaranteed to make you feel young and bright and attractive. This jumper will fit sizes 81cm to 92cm bust, since the rib is equally successful, either open or closed.

*The Australian Women's Weekly*, 25 March 1939.

**Materials:** 450g Patons Bluebell Merino 5 ply 100% Merino Wool, four 4.00mm and four 3.00mm double-pointed knitting needles (DPNs).
**Measurements:** Length from shoulder to lower edge, 47cm. Bust, 81–92cm *(102cm)*. Length of sleeve seam, 46cm.
**Tension:** 26 stitches to 10cm.

### THE FRONT

With two 3.00mm needles, cast on 84 *(110)* stitches and work 7.5cm in (k 1, p 1) rib. Change to 4.00mm needles and continue in (k 1, p 1) rib, but always knit into the back of the knit stitches, increasing one stitch at each end of the 7th and every following 8th row until there are 104 *(130)* stitches on the needle. Continue without further shaping until the work measures 32cm from the lower edge.

**Shape for the armhole**: Still knitting into the back of the knit stitches continue in rib and k 2 tog at both ends of the next and every alternate row until 60 *(86)* stitches remain.
Now increase once at both ends of the next and every following 4th row until there are 70 *(96)* stitches on the needle.

**Shape for the neck**: Work across 24 *(37)* stitches, cast off 22 stitches (very loosely), work to the end. Work on the last 24 *(37)* stitches, knitting 2 stitches tog at the neck edge on every row until 22 *(35)* stitches remain. In the next row increase once at the armhole edge, at the same time knitting 2 stitches tog at the neck edge, then in the following row k 2 tog at the neck edge (21-*34* stitches).
Work 2 rows without shaping.

**Shape the shoulder:** Cast off 5 *(9)* stitches at the armhole edge 3 times, then 6 *(7)* stitches once. Join in the wool at needle point and work on the remaining 24 *(37)* stitches to match the first side.

## THE BACK

Work exactly as given for the front until 60 *(86)* stitches remain. Now increase once at both ends of the next and every following 4th row until there are 72 *(98)* stitches on the needle. Work one row without shaping, then shape for the neck and shoulders thus: Work across 24 *(37)* stitches, cast off 24 stitches (very loosely), work to the end. Work on the last 24 *(37)* stitches, casting off 5 *(9)* stitches at the armhole edge 3 times, whilst at the same time on each return row k 2 tog at the neck edge until 6 *(7)* stitches remain. Cast off. Rejoin wool at needle point and work on the remaining 24 *(37)* stitches in the same way.

## THE COLLAR

Join the shoulder seams. Using a set of 3.00mm DPNs, with the right side of the work facing and starting at the left front shoulder, pick up and knit 120 stitches evenly around the neck (60 stitches each on front and back neckline). Distributing the stitches across three DPNs (40 stitches per needle) work in rounds of (k1,p1) rib (do not knit into the back of the knit stitches) for 4cm, ending at the left shoulder. **Next round:** Rib 25, cast off 10 stitches in rib, work in rib to the end of the round. Now work backwards and forwards in rib on the remaining stitches for 2.5cm, then change to 4.00mm needles and work a further 4cm in rib. Cast off loosely in the rib.

### THE SLEEVES

With 3.00mm needles cast on 44 *(48)* stitches and work 6.5cm in (k 1, p 1) rib (do not knit into the back of the knit stitches). Change to 4.00mm needles and continue in rib, but knit into the back of the knit stitches increasing once at each end of the 5th and every following 6th row until there are 74 *(78)* stitches on the needle. Continue without further shaping until the work measures 46cm from the lower edge.

**To shape the top:** K 2 tog at both ends of the next and every alternate row until 34 *(38)* stitches remain.

### TO MAKE UP

Press the work lightly under a damp cloth with a warm iron. Join the side and sleeve seams. Set in the sleeves, placing the centre of the cast-off stitches at the top to shoulder seams, and the two corners to the angles formed by the decreasings and increasings of the raglan armhole. Press all seams.

# Florence

A fascinating little jumper in which to go skittering hither and yon—at a moment's notice, perhaps. You'll love the new stitch.

*The Australian Women's Weekly*, 25 March 1939.

**Materials:** Long sleeves—400g Bendigo Woollen Mills Classic 3 ply wool (100% machine washable wool). Short sleeves—350g Bendigo Woollen Mills Classic 3 ply wool (100% machine washable wool); pair each 3.25mm and 2.75mm needles; 1 spare DPN.
**Measurements:** To fit 86cm bust. Length, shoulder to hem, 51cm. Long sleeve seam, 47cm. Short sleeve seam, 11.5cm.
**Tension:** 28 stitches and 40 rows to 10cm.

## BACK

Cast on 116 stitches on 3.25mm needles (do not work into back of stitches).
Work pattern as follows:
**1st row:** K 1 (for border), * p 6, k 6, * repeat * to * to last 7 stitches, p 6, k 1.
**2nd row:** K 1, * k 6, p 6, * repeat * to * to last 7 stitches, k 7.
Repeat last 2 rows once.
**5th row:** K 1, * p 6, sl next 3 stitches onto spare needle, bring to front of work, k 3, k 3 stitches from spare needle, * repeat * to * to last 7 stitches, p, 6, k, 1.
**6th, 8th and 9th rows:** as 2nd row.
**7th and 10th rows:** As 1st row.
Repeat 9th and 10th rows once.
**13th row:** K 1, * sl next 3 sts on spare needle, bring to front of work, k 3, k 3 stitches from spare needle, p 6, * repeat * to * to last 7 stitches, sl next 3 stitches on spare needle, bring to front of work, k 3, k 3 stitches from spare needle, k 1.
**14th and 16th rows:** As 1st row.
**15th row:** As 2nd row.
These 16 rows form the pattern for the back.
Work first row but with every stitch k in pattern the corresponding stitch of the cast on row to form a hem. Continue in pattern until work measures 15cm from bottom of hem.

Jersey with ribbed yoke and alternative instructions for short sleeves. The original yarn was Ramada Super Fingering wool in 3 ply; we updated it with Bendigo Woollen Mills Classic 3 ply in Seaquest.

Increase 1 stitch at each end of next and every 6th row until 128 stitches are on needle, working the extra stitches in pattern.
Continue on 128 stitches until work measures 36cm from bottom of hem (9 patterns worked, not including hem).

**Shape armholes:**
Cast off 6 stitches at beginning of next 2 rows.
K 2 tog at beginning of every row until 104 stitches remain.
Continue on 104 stitches, until armholes measure 11.5cm, measured straight up (12 patterns worked).

**Shape neck:**
** **Next row:** Pattern 43, turn, work back.
Pattern 39, turn, work back.
Pattern 35, turn, work back.
Pattern 31, turn, work back.
Pattern 27, turn, work back.**

**Shape shoulders:**
*** **Next row:** Cast off 7 stitches, pattern 20, turn, work back.
**Next row:** Cast off 7 stitches, pattern 13, turn, work back.
**Next row:** Cast off 7 stitches, pattern 6, turn, work back.
Cast off. ***
Join wool at centre to stitches left unworked and work to end of row.
Repeat from ** of other side, leaving the centre 50 stitches on spare needle.

**Yoke:**
With 2.75mm needles pick up 10 stitches along the side edge of shoulder shaping, k 50 stitches from spare needle, knitting twice into every 4th stitch, k up 10 stitches along other side of neck.
Work in k 2, p 2 rib for 22 rows. Cast off in rib.

## FRONT

Cast on 128 stitches on 3.25mm needles. Do not work into back of cast-on stitches.
Work pattern as follows:
**1st row:** K 1, * k 6, p 6 * repeat * to * to last 7 stitches, k 7.
**2nd row:** K 1, * p 6, k 6, * repeat * to * to last 7 stitches, p 6, k 1.
Repeat last 2 rows once.
**5th row:** K 1 * sl. next 3 stitches on spare needle, bring to front of work, k 3, k 3 stitches from spare needle, p 6 * repeat * to * to last 7 stitches, sl. next 3 stitches on spare needle, bring to front of work, k 3, k 3 stitches from needle, k 1.
**6th and 8th rows:** as 2nd row.
**7th row:** As 1st row.
**9th row:** K 1, *p 6, k 6 * repeat * to * to last 7 stitches, p 6, k 1.
**10th row:** K 1, * k 6, p 6, * repeat * to * to last 7 stitches, k 7.
Repeat last 2 rows once.
**13th row:** K 1, * p 6, sl. next 3 stitches on spare needle, bring to front of work, k 3 stitches, k 3 stitches from spare needle * repeat * to * to last 7 stitches, p 6, k 1.
**14th row:** As 10th row.
**15th row:** As 9th row.
**16th row:** As 10th row.
These 16 rows form the pattern for front.
Work the 1st row, but with every stitch k in pattern the corresponding stitch of the cast-on row, to form a hem.
Continue in pattern until work measures 15cm from bottom of hem.
Increase 1 stitch at each end of the next and every 6th row until 140 stitches are on needle.
Continue on 140 stitches until work measures 36cm from bottom of hem (9 patterns worked from hem).

**Shape armholes:**
Cast off 10 stitches at beginning of next 2 rows.
K 2 tog at beginning of every row until 104 stitches remain.
Continue on 104 stitches, until armholes measure 9cm, measured straight up (11 patterns).
**Shape neck** as for back from ** to **

Work 18 rows on 27 stitches.
**Shape shoulders** as for back.

**Yoke:**
With 2.75mm needles, pick up 21 stitches down side of neck shaping, k across centre 50 stitches, knitting twice into every 4th stitch, pick up 24 stitches along other side of neck.
Work k 2, p 2, rib for 22 rows. Cast off in rib.

## LONG SLEEVES

Cast on 56 stitches on 3.25mm needles. Work in pattern as given for back for 16 rows, then make hem as given for back. Continue in pattern until work measures 7.5cm from bottom of hem. Increase 1 stitch at each end of next and every 8th row until 92 stitches are on needle.

Continue on 92 stitches until work measures 47cm from bottom of hem (12 pattern repeats). Cast off 2 stitches at beginning of every row until 28 stitches remain. Cast off.

## SHORT SLEEVES

Cast on 92 stitches on 2.75mm needles. Work in k 2, p 2 rib for 5cm. Change to 3.25mm needles and work pattern as for back for 6.5cm from bottom of hem. Shape top as for long sleeves.

## TO MAKE UP

Lightly press work with hot iron over damp cloth. Sew up side, shoulder and sleeve seams. Sew sleeves into armholes.

# 20th-century knitting

Understanding the culture of early twentieth-century knitting in Australia allows a window into society, revealing frugality, family and fashion, and shifting cultural ties.

Knitting was given a boost in Australia by keen practitioner Queen Victoria, and interest in the craft and in her iconic feminine domesticity carried through to the early twentieth century.

During the war years, knitting was a popular activity with patriotic associations encouraging people to knit for the soldiers. Photographs show women and children knitting busily and men posing with knitting paraphernalia. Indeed, knitting was no longer a purely feminine pursuit. Some Australian men learned to knit as part of their jobs. Prison warders, for instance, were sometimes required to teach prisoners to knit.

From the 1920s, Patons & Baldwins in Tasmania produced excellent handknitting yarns. Wool was cheap, and knitting for the family made economic sense. In the 1930s, women's magazines published knitting patterns with a domestic focus: garments and accessories for the entire family, and homewares such as tea cosies and toys. In times of scarcity, people created attractive garments with Fair Isle patterns that used only small amounts of wool in each colour.

Knitting was also a fashion statement. French designers Coco Chanel and Anny Blatt popularised woollen jumpers and jersey dresses in Europe, prompting a jumper craze in the 1920s. Women embraced this as an escape from formal, prewar dress codes. Fair Isle jumpers became especially popular after the Prince of Wales wore one during a golf event in 1922.

The popularity of handknitted clothing peaked between the 1930s and the 1950s. Publications reflected the prevailing vogue of the day, and Australian magazines tantalised women with the glamour of international film stars and fashion. A strong American presence in Australia during the Second World War meant an influx of new ideas about consumption and fashion. America soon replaced Europe as a major cultural influence. The argyle pattern on page 41 is touted as having American style, while the youthful Sandra cardigan on page 26 was 'created in Hollywood'.

Cover of *The Australian Women's Weekly* from 6 May 1944, the patriotic colours a sign of the times.

The Australian
WOMEN'S WEEKLY
SOLD EVERY WEEK
May 6, 1944
Registered in Australia for transmission by post as a newspaper.
PRICE
3D
KNITTING INSTRUCTIONS
FOR
FOUR SMART GARMENTS

Directions for knitting the checked Argyle pattern are given in both the pattern instructions and the graph. The original yarn was Lincoln Mills 'Daphne' crochet wool 100% wool yarn. This was approximately a fingering weight or 4 ply yarn.

Originally worked in black and white, we've updated it in cream and apricot 4 ply wool. This is a rare vintage pattern that gives instructions for a range of three sizes.

# Barbara

A smart new American fashion, the argyle jacket is regarded as high fashion for late afternoon and after-dark wear.

*The Australian Women's Weekly*, 1 April 1953.

**Materials:** 450g (total) Millpost Merino 4 ply in cream and apricot—300g light colour, 150g dark colour; pair each 3.25mm and 2.75mm knitting needles (long).
**Measurements:** To fit 81 (*86*-92) bust. Length from top of shoulder (excluding band) 47 (*47.5*-53.5)cm; length of side seam (excluding band) 26 (*26*-31)cm; width across sleeve at upper arm 20 (*21*-21.5)cm.
**Tension:** 30 stitches and 36 rows to 10cm.

## BACK

Using light wool and 3.25mm needles, commencing at lower edge cast on 133 (*141*-149) stitches. Use the chart on p47 as a guide. Work in stocking stitch starting at B (*B*-A) thus: Follow chart across, then omitting centre stitch work back to beginning for other half of design. Work in this manner until C is reached, then work from A to C twice more.

**Sleeve shaping:** Keeping continuity of pattern Cast on 6 (*6*-7) stitches at the end of next row 14 (*12*-14) times.
Cast on 0 (*9*-0) stitches at the end of next row 0 (*2*-0) times.
There are now 217 (*231*-247) stitches on the needle.
Work in pattern without further increase until work measures 13 (*13.5*-14)cm from last increase row, i.e. 45 (*47*-49) rows.
**Top of sleeves and shoulder shaping:** Cast off 13 (*13*-15) stitches at the beginning of the next 10 (*8*-8) rows. Cast off 12 (*14*-14) stitches at the beginning of the next 4 (*6*-6) rows.
Change to 2.75mm needles and work in k 1, p 1 rib over the rem. 39 (*43*-43) stitches for 5cm.
Cast off in rib.

## LEFT FRONT

Commencing at lower edge with light wool and 3.25mm needles, cast on 67 (*71*-75) stitches. Work in stocking stitch commencing at B (*B*-A): Follow chart until C is reached, then repeat from A to C twice more.

**Sleeve shaping:** Cont. in pattern casting on 6 (*6*-7) stitches at end of next purl row 7 (*6*-7) times, then 0 (*9*-0) stitches 0 (*1*-0) times. There are now 109 (*116*-124) stitches. Work without further increase, until work measures 10 (*10*-11)cm from last increase row ending at front edge, i.e. 37 (*37*-39) rows.

**Neck shaping:** Cast off 2 stitches at the beginning of next row, then cast off 2 stitches at the same edge on every alternate row following 10 (*11*-11) times in all, and at the same time when work measures 13 (*13.5*-14)cm from last increase row ending at side edge, shape top of sleeve and shoulder as follows:

Cast off 13 (*13*-15) stitches at the beginning of next row and at same edge 5 (*4*-4) times in all. Cast off 12 (*14*-16) stitches at same edge 2 (*3*-3) times.

## RIGHT FRONT

Work to correspond with left front, reversing shapings and chart.

## BANDS

**Back:** With right side of work facing and using 2.75mm needles and light wool, pick up and knit along lower edge of back 133 (*141*-149) stitches Work in k 1, p 1 rib for 5cm. Cast off in rib.

**Right front:** With right side of work facing and using 2.75mm needles and light wool, pick up and knit along lower edge 67 (*71*-75) stitches, k 4 more times in last stitch (front edge). Pick up and knit along front edge to neck 134 (*134*-134) stitches, k 4 more times in last stitch (corner of neck), pick up and knit along neck shaping 30 (*33*-33) stitches. There are now 239 (*246*-250) stitches on needle.
Work in k 1, p 1 rib for 5cm. Cast off in rib.

**Left front:** Work to correspond with right front. Join shoulder and top of sleeve seam.

## CUFFS

With right side of work facing and using 2.75mm needles and light wool, pick up and knit around cuff edge 76 (*80*-84) stitches. Work in k 1, p 1 rib for 5cm.
Cast off in rib.

## TO MAKE UP

Press all parts under a damp cloth. Join side and underarm seams. Fold all bands in half and sew cast off edges along first row of ribbing on wrong side.

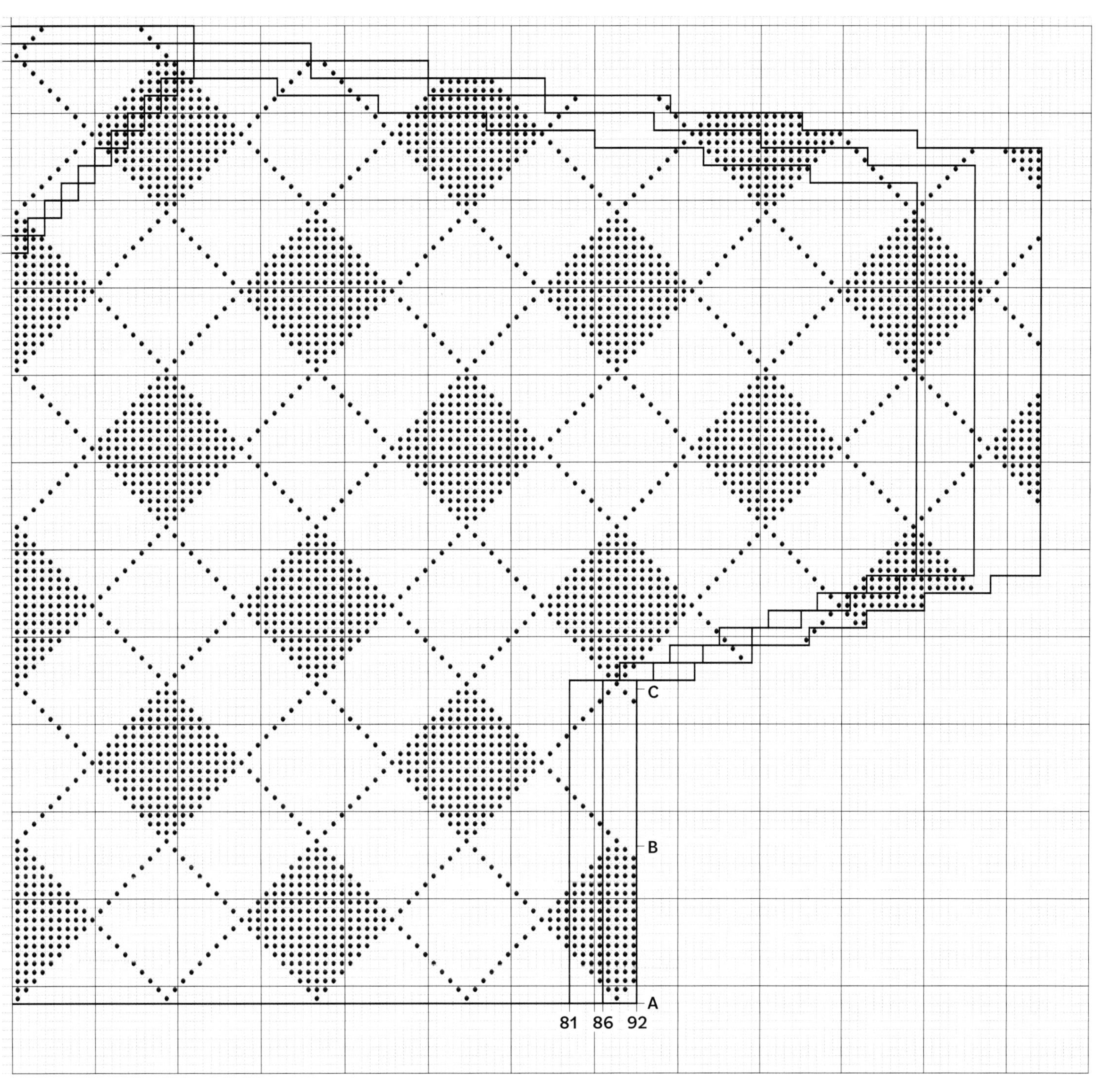


**Light** **Dark**

Chart to be used in conjunction with the knitting instructions.

Directions are given for three sizes: 81cm, *86cm* and 92cm bust measurements.

# Dorothea

To make you slender as a jonquil's stem, Vienna is behind 'Dorothea' with her snowy-white, double-breasted cardigan, a-sparkle with crystal buttons.

*The Australian Women's Weekly*, 25 March 1939.

**Materials:** 125g Australian Alpaca Barn 'Divine' (74% baby alpaca, 26% silk) in Champagne. 12 buttons. 1 pair each 4.00mm and 3.25mm needles. 4.00mm crochet hook.
**Measurements:** To fit 85cm bust. Length, shoulder to hem, 52cm, sleeve seam, 47cm.
**Tension:** 22 stitches and 30 rows to 10cm. Work into back of all cast-on stitches. Pattern is worked in stocking stitch throughout.

## BACK

Cast on 78 stitches on 3.25mm needles. Work k 2, p 2 rib for 26 rows.
Change to 4.00mm needles and stocking stitch, increasing 1 stitch each end of next and every 12th row until 90 stitches are on needle.
Continue on 90 stitches until work measures 35cm from cast on.
**Shape armholes:** Cast off 4 stitches at beginning of next 2 rows.
K 2 tog at each end of next 6 rows (70 stitches).
Continue on 70 stitches and work 12 rows in stocking stitch without further shaping.
Continuing on 4.00mm needles, work 32 rows k2, p2 rib.
**Shape shoulders:** Continuing in rib, cast off 6 stitches at beginning of next 8 rows. Cast off.

## RIGHT FRONT

Cast on 50 stitches on 3.25mm needles. Work k 2, p 2 rib for 10 rows.
**Next row:** Make buttonhole (right side): k 2, p 2, cast off 3 stitches, p 1, k 2, p 2, k 2, p 1, cast off 3 stitches, rib to end of row.
**Next row:** (wrong side): rib until last 12 st, cast on 3 stitches, k 1, p 2, k 2, p 2, k 1, cast on 3 stitches, rib to end.
Work 14 rows rib (26 rows in total).

Although Anny Blatt yarns are still available, the 'Kurly' wool that was recommended for this cardigan is no longer in production. We chose to replace it with an alpaca yarn for its glamorous softness and fluffy texture. We also left out the bands from the original design to make a more classic and elegant look.

Change to 4.00mm needles and continue in stocking stitch increasing 1 stitch at side edge of next and every 12th row until there are 56 stitches on needle and at the same time working buttonholes, starting on the next row and then every 27th and 28th rows.

**Buttonhole rows (stocking stitch):**

**Next row (right side):** K 4, cast off 3 stitches, k 8, cast off 3 stitches, work to end.

**Next row (wrong side):** P until last 12 stitches, cast on 3 stitches, p 8, cast on 3 stitches, work to end. Continue until work measures 35cm from cast on, ending at side edge.

Note: by the time you reach the armhole shaping, you should have worked 3 sets of buttonholes - one set in rib section and two more sets in stocking stitch section.

**Shape armhole:**

Cast off 4 stitches, work to end of row.

**Next row (right side):** K to last 3 stitches, k 2 tog, k 1.

**Next row (wrong side):** K 1, p 2 tog, work to end.

Work these 2 rows three times (46 stitches). Work 12 rows in stocking stitch without further

shaping, but including buttonhole rows as described above.
Continuing on 4.00mm needles, work k 2, p 2 rib until sixth set of button holes has been worked, ending at front edge.
Work 2 rows in rib.
**Shape neck:** Cast off 16 stitches, rib to end.
**Next row (wrong side):** Rib to last 3 stitches, k 2 tog tbl, k 1.
**Next row (right side):** K 1, sl1k1psso, rib to end.
Work these 2 rows three times (24 stitches).
Shape shoulder: Cast off 6 stitches at beginning (sleeve edge) of next and following alternate rows, three times. Cast off.

## LEFT FRONT

Work to match right front, omitting buttonholes.
Cast on 50 stitches using 3.25mm needles. Work 26 rows in k 2, p 2 rib.
Change to 4.00mm needles and continue in stocking stitch increasing 1 stitch at side edge of next and every 12th row until there are 56 stitches on needle
Continue until work measures 35cm from cast-on edge., ending at side edge.
Cast off 4 stitches, work to end of row.
**Next row (wrong side):** P to last 3 stitches, p 2 tog tbl, k 1.
**Next row (right side):** k 1, k 2 tog, work to end.
Work these 2 rows three times (46 stitches).
Work 12 rows in stocking stitch without further shaping.
Continuing on 4.00mm needles, work k 2, p 2 rib until length matches right front to neck shaping ending at front edge.
Cast off 16 stitches, rib to end.
**Next row (right side):** Rib to last 3 stitches, k 2 tog, k 1.
**Next row (wrong side):** K 1, s1k1psso, rib to end.
Work these 2 rows three times (24 stitches).
Cast off 6 stitches at beginning (sleeve edge) of next and following alt rows, three times. Cast off.

## SLEEVES (BOTH ALIKE)

Cast on 40 stitches on 3.25mm needles.
Work k 2, p 2 rib for 16 rows.
Change to 4.00mm needles and stocking stitch, increasing 1 stitch at each end of 9th and following 8th rows until 60 stitches are on needle.
Continue without further shaping until sleeve measures 47cm, ending with a wrong side row.
Cast off 4 stitches at beginning of next 2 rows.
K 2 tog at each end of next 6 rows (40 stitches).
Continue in stocking stitch, decreasing 1 stitch at each end of 5th and following 4th rows, four times in total; then at each end of alternate rows, four times in total (24 stitches).
Cast off 4 stitches at beginning of next four rows. Cast off.

## TO MAKE UP

Press stocking stitch part of work on wrong side with hot iron over damp cloth.
Sew up shoulder, side and sleeve seams.
Using 4.00mm crochet hook, work 1 row DC up right front edge, around neck and down left front.
Sew sleeves into armholes, easing gently to fit.
Sew buttons on left front to match buttonholes.

Note: as the knitted fabric is very light, if the buttons are heavy you can add a few press studs to help the front edge and neckline keep its shape.

# Yarn tales

Knitting yarns recommended for the patterns in this book are mainly wool, as this natural fibre has been long prized for its elasticity, warmth and durability. Other animal and plant fibres can also be spun to use as yarn, giving different properties to the finished fabric. In the second half of the twentieth century, synthetic fibres that emulated some of the properties of wool or cotton began to be mass produced.

**Wool**

Wool comes from sheep and is prized for its elasticity, strength and warmth. Like all animal hair, the strands of wool are covered with microscopic scales that can catch and help bond the fibres together; this is particularly useful in felting (and it's why you shouldn't wash woollens in hot water or tumble-dry them).

**Other animal fibres**

Mohair and cashmere come from goats: vicuña and alpaca from the animals whose names they bear; and angora from fluffy rabbits. In addition, people have been known to spin the fur of long-haired dogs or cats and even human hair.

**Silk**

Usually blended with wool or other fibres for the purposes of knitting, silk is a lustrous, smooth fibre that comes from the cocoon of the silk moth (*Bombyx mori*). It is about twice as strong as steel and has all the desirable qualities of other animal fibres, although it is not as elastic as wool. Plied together with other fibres, it adds a luxurious element to a yarn.

**Cotton**

Plant fibres such as cotton have some elasticity and allow the body to breathe, so they are suitable for clothing designed for warmer weather than woollens, which retain heat. Cotton comes from the seed pods of the *Gossypium* species; the seeds must be combed out before the fibre can be carded and spun. Cotton has little elasticity, but it can be blended with Lycra or elastane.

**Rayon**

Rayon is a manufactured fibre, but it is made of cellulose, which is the main ingredient in cotton, so rayon has many of the same properties: it is soft, smooth, absorbent and comfortable .

**Bamboo**

If you're looking for an environmentally friendly fibre, bamboo is one of the best. In recent years it has overtaken cotton in popularity for knitting because it has many of the same properties as that fibre but it is more sustainable: it requires less water to grow and can be harvested without killing the plant, which immediately regrows from its underground stem.

This photograph, taken by Wolfgang Sievers, shows a man winding wool at Yarra Falls Limited in Melbourne's Abbotsford in 1960.

### Linen and hemp

Linen fibres come from the stems of the flax plant (*Linum usitatissimum*) and hemp from *Cannabis sativa* (a non-psychoactive form of the marijuana plant). These fibres can be used for knitting, although they are less elastic than cotton and bamboo. Both linen and hemp fibres are strong (stronger than cotton), absorbent and comfortable to wear, especially in hot weather. They are often blended with wool or a synthetic fibre to give a more pleasing drape and stretch to the knitted fabric.

### Synthetic and art fibres

Manufactured fibres that can be used for knitting include rayon, nylon, polyester (made from a petrochemical base) and acrylic. They emulate some of the qualities of wool, although they tend to be less durable. On the plus side, they come in many brilliant colours and textures that wool can't maintain, and they are the source of some fun yarns such as eyelash yarn, ribbon yarn and glitter yarn. Paper and plastic yarns are also available: these are not really suited to use in garments, but can be a fun alternative to play with.

# Margaret

This waistcoat has been designed by Margaret Eton in response to a request from many knitters for a simple woollen blouse to take the place of a silk one, and to button down the front rather than slip over the head. It may be worn under a tweed coat or jacket, or as a top jacket if preferred.

*The Argus*, 7 May 1936.

**Materials:** 400g Bendigo Woollen Mills Luxury 4 ply in Stone. For the checks, 25g Bendigo Woollen Mills Luxury 4 ply in Baby Blossom, one pair 3.25 *(3.75)*mm needles.
**Measurements:** Length of jacket back from bottom edge to shoulder, 46cm *(48cm)*. Length of jacket from bottom edge to underarm, 25cm *(30cm)*. Length of sleeve to underarm, 46cm. To fit 81cm *(92cm)* bust.
**Tension:** 28 stitches and 46 rows to 10cm over garter stitch using 3.25mm needles.
**Note:** The entire garment is knitted in garter stitch. Slip the first and purl the last stitch in each row in all the knitting.

## RIGHT FRONT

Cast on two stitches, knit into the back of these stitches. Knit twice into both stitches.
**Next row:** Knit, knitting twice into the second-last stitch.
**Next row:** Knit, knitting twice into the second and second-last stitch. Repeat the last two rows until the stitches number 29.
**Next row:** Cast on 25 stitches. Knit into the back of these and across the 29 stitches on the needle.
**Next row:** Knit, knitting twice into the second stitch, repeat the increasing at this end seven times.
**Next row:** To make a buttonhole at the shaped side knit 2, cast off 4, knit to end of row.
**Next row:** Cast on 4 stitches where the cast-off stitches are.
**Next row:** Knit, knitting into the back of the cast-on stitches.
Repeat the buttonhole thus every 26th row until there are 6 buttonholes. When the second buttonhole is made, ° starting from the buttonhole end, knit 2 rows in the contrast colour, then change back to the original wool. ° Repeat this at every succeeding 52nd row.

During the Depression, many women could no longer afford the luxury of fibres like silk, increasing demand for woollen alternatives. Originally knitted in 3 ply wool, we kept the spirit of the design by knitting this in a 4 ply machine-washable 100% wool yarn in muted tones. The sample was knitted one size larger than the pattern simply by using 3.75mm needles instead of the recommended 3.25mm.

When the work measures 10cm from the cast-on stitches, at the opposite side from the buttonholes, knit twice into the second-last stitch. Repeat the increasing every 10th row until there are 8 increasings.
When the stitches are cast off for the 6th buttonhole the work should measure 25cm *(30cm)* from the cast-on stitches at the bottom at the shaped side. Cast off 12 stitches for the armhole. At this end k 2 tog every 4th row 4 times.
Then, at the lapel side, k 6, knit twice into the next stitch, knit to end.
Repeat the increasings every 10th row until there are 6 increasings. When 72 rows from the cast-off stitches are knitted, on the opposite side from the armhole, cast off 24 stitches to make the lapel. Continue for 24 rows.
When it is time to knit the contrast stripes (° to °) start the contrast colour 20 stitches in from the buttonhole edge to allow for the lapels.
* Cast off 10 stitches at the armhole end of the next row. Knit 1 row.* Repeat * to *, and cast off.

### LEFT FRONT

The left side is knitted to correspond with the right side, omitting the buttonholes.
To begin, cast on 2 stitches, knit into the back of these stitches. Knit twice into both stitches.
**Next row:** Knit, knitting twice into the second-last stitch.
**Next row:** Knit, knitting twice into the second and second-last stitch. Repeat the last two rows until the stitches number 28.
**Next row:** Cast on 26 stitches. Knit into the back of these and across the 28 stitches on the needle, increasing in second-last stitch.
**Next row:** Knit, knitting twice into the second-last stitch, repeat the increasing at this end 7 times.

### THE BACK

Cast on 90 stitches, knit into the back of each stitch. Continue in garter stitch, slipping the first stitch and purling the last in each row, as for the front. When 52 rows are knitted, knit 2 rows in contrast yarn, repeat every 52nd row.

When 10cm are knitted increase 1 stitch each end of every 10th row.

When the work measures 25cm *(30cm)*, cast off 12 stitches at the beginning of the next two rows. Continue without further decreasing for 92 rows from the cast-off stitches.

Cast off 10 stitches at the beginning of the next 4 rows. Cast off.

### THE SLEEVES

Cast on 56 stitches, knit into the back of each stitch, knit for 9cm. Increase 1 stitch each end of every 10th row until the stitches number 92. Continue until the work measures 46cm.

At the beginning of the next two rows, cast off 12 stitches. Knit 2 together at each end every fourth row 14 times.

Knit 4 rows without decreasing. Cast off 1 stitch at the beginning of every succeeding row until the stitches number 34.

Cast off 3 stitches at the beginning of the next 6 rows. Cast off remaining stitches.

### TO MAKE UP

Join the shoulder seams. Starting 10 stitches from the edge of the lapel; pick up the stitches round the neck for the collar; these should number 96. Knit for 28 rows and cast off.

Pick up the stitches down the front edges. Knit 2 rows and cast off. Pick up the 14 stitches on the edge of the collar, knit 2 rows, and cast off.

The vertical lines are embroidered in chain stitch, with the contrast wool, and are ruled on in pencil 10cm apart: starting from the centre edge rule the first line 6.5cm from this. Then when the garment is worn, the lines are symmetrical.

Likewise the back: fold the piece in half and rule 5cm from this fold towards the outside as a guide for the first line. Join the side and sleeve seams, and the sleeves are put in seam to seam.

# Vintage styles and yarns

In the 1930s, knitwear designers began introducing features such as bobbles into knitting designs for visual interest. Ribbing, cabling and stitch variations were added for textural effects. *The Australian Women's Weekly* went as far as describing purl and plain as 'stereotyped'. Readers were encouraged to be adventurous and follow the latest European fashions. Judith on page 18, uses 'a new twisted rib', while Florence on page 38 is described 'with the hallmark of Paris'.

These knitting designs from the 25 March 1939 edition of *The Australian Women's Weekly* feature textural effects and slim waists typical of the era.

The 1930s have been called 'the great age of Hollywood'. Film stars such as Lana Turner and Ava Gardner popularised the snug, fitted look that began influencing women's knitwear from the late 1930s and into the 1940s. To encourage a trim look, fashion designers focused on the shoulder, using capes and puffed sleeves to draw the eye upwards, which resulted in a slimming effect at the waist. Dorothea (on page 48) promises to 'make you slender as a jonquil's stem'!

Patons was a well-known yarn manufacturer at this time and sold a wide range of knitting yarns, including Viyella wool, which was guaranteed unshrinkable in seawater. Pagoda crepe was launched as a new wool yarn with a crimped finish, incorporating silk in its ply. Crochet wool was used for producing striking stitch effects. Some Patons' 2 ply yarns were blended with angora and nylon to produce a very fine fabric with a cashmere feel.

Vintage 2 ply and 3 ply yarns were thicker than their modern equivalents. Today 4 ply is sometimes substituted for them in order to maintain the correct stitch count and tension; however, using modern 2 and 3 ply yarns will result in the finer, softer feel of the old garments. Modern 2 ply and 3 ply yarns, being very smooth, are also recommended for babywear.

In recent years, there has been something of a trend in knitting circles towards using super-thick yarns and very large knitting needles (with a diameter of 1cm or more), which make for very quick knits as well as interesting textures. When using the finer classic yarns recommended for the patterns in this book, the interest comes from the intricate stitch patterns and tailored garment shapes.

# Helen

You'll agree this jumper is lovely enough to set every knitting needle a-flying! Featuring the new, wide shoulder effect, this delightful diagonal-rib jumper combines two colours very effectively. The back, front, and sleeves are knitted up to a certain point, joined together, then all the stitches are picked up on four needles and the yoke is worked round and round as you would for a stocking. Use two needles to make the body and sleeves.

*The Australian Women's Weekly*, 13 April 1935.

**Materials:** 250g Inca Spun Heritage sock yarn (55% fine merino wool, 20% alpaca, 25% nylon) 4 ply (body and sleeves); 100g Indiecita 100% baby alpaca 4 ply in tangerine (yoke). Five 4.5mm double-pointed knitting needles, crochet hook.

**Measurements:** Bust 81cm, length 52cm, sleeve seam 45cm.

**Tension:** 26 stitches and 30 rows to 10cm.

### FRONT AND BACK—BOTH ALIKE

Cast on 92 stitches.

**1st row:** *K 2, p 1, repeat from * to end of row, finishing with k 2.

**2nd row:** *P 2, k 1, repeat from * to end of row, finishing with p 2.

Repeat these 2 rows 12 times.

Continue, working in the following pattern:

**1st row:** K 8, *p 1, k 1, p 1, k 8, repeat from * to end of row, finishing with k 4.

**2nd row:** P 4, * k 1, p 1, k 1, p 8, repeat from * to end, finishing with p 8.

**3rd row:** K 7, * p 1, k 1, p 1, k 8, repeat from * to end, finishing with k 5.

**4th row:** P 5, * k 1, p 1, k 1, p 8, repeat from * to end, finishing with p 7.

**5th row:** K 6, * p 1, k 1, p 1, k 8, repeat from * to end, finishing with k 6.

**6th row:** P 6, * k 1, p 1, k 1, p 8, repeat from * to end, finishing with p 6.

**7th row:** K 5, * p 1, k 1, p 1, k 8, repeat from * to end, finishing with k 7.

**8th row:** P 7, * k 1, p 1, k 1, p 8, repeat from * to end, finishing with p 5.

**9th row:** K 4, * p 1, k 1, p 1, k 8, repeat from * to end, finishing with k 8.

**10th row:** P 8, * k 1, p 1, k 1, p 8, repeat from * to end, finishing with p 4.

**11th row:** K 3, * p 1, k 1, p 1, k 8, repeat from * to end, finishing with p 1.

As you can see, this enchanting jumper will be equal to any occasion—it is an aristocrat in design and will remain one throughout its charming life. Red and white were used for the original model, but, of course, any colour scheme could be used. Two blues, or chocolate and cream, would look equally effective.

Viyella wool in 4 ply was used for the original, and we've updated it with a combination of tweedy blended yarn for the body and a vibrant alpaca yarn for the yoke.

PETROV.

**12th row:** K 1, * p 8, k 1, p 1, k 1, repeat from * to end, finishing with p 3.
**13th row:** K 2, *p 1, k 1, p 1, k 8. Repeat from * to end, finishing with k 1.
**14th row:** P 1, k 1, * p 8, k 1, p 1, k 1, repeat from * to end, finishing with p 2.
**15th row:** K 1, * p 1, k 1, p 1, k 8, repeat from * to end, finishing with p 1.
**16th row:** * K 1, p 1, k 1, p 8, repeat from * to end, finishing with p 1.
**17th row:** * P 1, k 1, p 1, k 8, repeat from * to end, finishing with k 1.
**18th row:** P 1, * k 1, p 1, k 1, p 8, repeat from * to end, finishing with k 1.
**19th row:** K 1, p 1, * k 8, p 1, k 1, p 1, repeat from * to end, finishing with k 2.
**20th row:** P 2, * k 1, p 1, k 1, p 8, repeat from * to end, finishing with p 1.
**21st row:** K 1, * k 8, p 1, k 1, p 1, repeat from * to end, finishing with k 3.
**22nd row:** P 3, * k 1, p 1, k 1, p 8, repeat from * to end, finishing with a k 1.
Repeat these 22 rows till work measures 34cm from beginning, then decrease at each end of every row till 82 stitches remain.
Work 31 stitches in pattern, put on spare needle, cast off 20 stitches, and work remaining 31 stitches, keeping in pattern.
Cast off 12 at neck end, continue to last 2 stitches, p these tog. Working on the remaining 18 stitches:
**Next row:** K 2 tog, pattern to end.
**Next row:** Pattern to last 2 stitches, p 2 tog
**Next row:** K 2 tog, pattern to end.
Repeat last 2 rows once more, then cast off remaining 13 stitches. Work other side to match.

## SLEEVE

Cast on 40 stitches. Work 24 rows in rib as for bottom of jumper. Now work in pattern but increase at both ends of every 10th row 10 times. (60 stitches on needle.) Now decrease at each end of every row till 50 stitches remain.
Work 20 stitches in pattern, cast off middle 10 stitches, and work 20 stitches in pattern.
**Next row:** P 2 together, pattern to end.
**Next row:** Cast off 2, pattern to end.
Repeat these 2 rows twice. Cast off. Join yarn to remaining stitches on needle and work shaping to match the other side of the sleeve.
Work another sleeve.

## YOKE

The yoke is worked in a rib of k 1, p 1, with a pattern forming holes every third row. Care must be taken when decreasing so that the continuity of the rib is not broken. The holes come directly one above the other, so if you find 2 plain or 2 purl stitches at the end of the needle together, plain or purl them as the case may be, the odd stitch will be taken in with the next decrease.
Carefully sew jumper together, then with the 4.5mm DPNs and contrasting yarn, pick up 64 stitches along front of jumper; with another needle pick up 44 stitches along top of sleeve. For back, pick up another 64 stitches using a 3rd needle, and another 44 stitches along other sleeve on a 4th needle. Now work in rounds.
**1st round:** K 1, p 1 all round, decreasing at end of each needle by knitting last stitch with the first stitch of next needle.
**2nd round:** K 1, p 1, decrease as for 1st round.
**3rd round:** *K 1, p 1, k 2 tog, make 1 by bringing yarn in front of needle. Repeat from * to end.
Work 8 repeats of the following three rounds (giving 9 rows of holes and 27 rounds in total):
**4th round:** K 1, p 1 all round (no decrease).
**5th round:** K 1, p 1 all round, decreasing at end of each needle by knitting last stitch together with the first stitch of next needle.
**6th round:** *K 1, p 1, k 2 tog, make 1 by bringing yarn in front of needle. Repeat from * to end.
Work 2 more rounds, decreasing on both.
Cast off.
With main colour yarn and 4.5mm crochet hook, work a chain long enough to go round jumper at bottom of yoke. Work a single crochet in each stitch and sew round.
Make another and sew at neck.

# Machines take over

Although the craft of handknitting has continued to be practised throughout the twentieth century and into the third millennium, the past 200 years have changed it completely.

Men operate machinery at the Bruck Mills in Wangaratta, Victoria, in this 1950 Wolfgang Sievers photograph.

Australia's wool industry benefitted in many ways from the industrial revolution of the eighteenth and nineteenth centuries. Inventions and technological advances meant that new forces could be harnessed to make processes such as shearing and wool processing more efficient. From the late 1800s onwards, steam-powered equipment and internal combustion engines meant that sheep could be washed in warm water to better clean their wool and make shearing faster and more productive. Wool could be pressed more effectively and packed more compactly. Fencing, breeding, disease control and transport were also transformed. These improvements enabled Australia's wool industry to thrive and compete in world markets. Sheep and wool industries both profited, with flow-on effects for knitting in terms of the quality and availability of yarn.

Australian textile mills began using water- and steam-powered machinery for spinning and weaving. These mills produced practical items, such as blankets, and woollen fabric for clothing, such as tweed. Some knitting yarn was produced, but the emphasis was on the production of clothing and cloth for sewing into clothes. Textiles were also produced at home. Yarn for knitting could be spun at home or unpicked from old garments and reused.

In the 1950s, knitting machines made an appearance in the home, but handknitting continued as a practical and popular craft.

# The world wide knitting web

The twenty-first century revival of knitting received a boost from the proliferation of websites, social networking sites and podcasts that have enabled knitters around the world to connect with each other, sharing their creations, patterns and techniques.

This business owner is offering her employee knitting guidance by way of a smart phone.

Knitters commonly use the internet for finding patterns, getting new project ideas and purchasing yarn and supplies. The most popular websites are social media sites, followed by yarn purchasing sites and also video sites that host short clips showing how to do certain stitches and techniques.

Knitting apps are available to do everything from organising projects and patterns to keeping track of yarns and tools.

Popular knitting website Ravelry.com has a library of patterns and photographs, allowing knitters to connect with each other and form local or interest-based knitting groups. The founders of Ravelry also regularly set challenges that knitters can participate in if they wish.

In the lead up to the 2006 Winter Olympics in Torino, author and knitting blogger Stephanie Pearl-McPhee (known as the Yarn Harlot) used social media to challenge her followers to begin a knitting project during the Olympics opening ceremony and have it finished 16 days later before the Olympic flame was extinguished. By the end of the first day, almost 4000 knitters had entered the challenge. A 'gold medal' was designed for those who excelled!

If you're looking for inspiration, supplies or friendly challenges, visit some of the popular sites for yourself: ravelry.com, Instagram.com (search for #knitstagram to get started), or try online stores such as morrisandsons.com.au or purlsoho.com.

# Men

Men's daywear in the early to mid-twentieth century was divided into two categories: business (or workwear) and sport. Sportswear was not activewear as we would think of it today: it was more a relaxed version of the business suit. Traditional cricketing flannels and vests was suitable casual attire for all sorts of 'manly' activities such as tennis, golf, fishing and cycling. Most of the patterns in this book are in this style.

In the workplace, three-piece suits were often complemented by a knitted vest or jumper in cooler weather, though a man in the 1930s or 1940s would never be considered properly dressed if he wore only a jumper. Any knitwear for business attire had to be fitted and made in fine yarn for wearing under a suit jacket. The range of yarns available was limited, so variety of style was a result of interesting stitch patterns and, occasionally, features such as a collar.

It was usually assumed that the knitting itself would be done by the man's wife, mother or even sister. Though some men knew how to knit, they were certainly not the norm. Today, many men and boys take up the needles to create their own garments and add signature style to their wardrobe.

The simple, but effective, pattern was worked out by knitting experts to ensure comfort and fit. The original was knitted in 3 ply wool; our updated version is made in a larger size by adding stitches to front and back *(shown in brackets)*.

# Jack

Here is a pattern for a pullover in which the man of the house will be warm and well dressed in the office, on the golf course, or after a game of tennis.

*The Sunday Mail*, 27 July 1952.

**Materials:** 350g Bendigo Woollen Mills Classic 3 ply in Silver; pair each of 3.25mm, 2.75mm and 2.00mm needles.
**Measurements:** Length from top of shoulder, 62cm *(65cm)*; width all round underarm, 96.5cm *(102cm)*.
**Tension:** 32 stitches and 36 rows to 10cm.

## BACK

Using 2.75mm needles, cast on 132 *(160)* stitches.
**1st row:** k 2, * p 1, k 1, repeat from * to end. Repeat 1st row 38 times.
**40th row:** k 2, * (p 1, k 1) 4 times, p 1, increase once in next stitch, repeat from * to last 10 stitches (p 1, k 1) 5 times (144 stitches) *(increase 16 stitches evenly across row—176 stitches)*.
**1st pattern row:** Using 3.25mm needles, knit.
**2nd row:** k 4, p 8, * k 8, p 8, repeat from * to last 4 stitches, k 4.
**3rd row:** p 3, k 2 together, k 3, pick up thread between stitches and knit into back, then into front of loop (increase 2 sts), k 3, sl 1, k 1, psso, * p 6, k 2 together, k 3, pick up thread between stitches and knit into back, then into front of loop, k 3, sl, 1, k 1, psso, repeat from * to last 3 stitches, p 3.
**4th row:** k 3, p 10, * k 6, p 10, repeat from * to last 3 stitches, k 3.
**5th row:** p 2, k 2 together, k 3, pick up thread between stitches and knit through back of loop (this will be termed increase 1 throughout), k 2, increase 1, k 3, sl 1, k 1, psso, * p 4, k 2 together, k 3, increase 1, k 2, increase 1, k 3, sl 1, k 1, psso, repeat from * to last 2 stitches, p 2.
**6th row:** k 2, p 12, * k 4, p 12, repeat from * to last 2 stitches, k 2.
**7th row:** p 1, K 2 together, k 3, increase 1, k 4, increase 1, k 3, sl 1, k 1, psso, * p 2, k 2 together, k 3, increase 1, k 4, increase 1, k 3, sl 1, k 1, psso,

repeat from * to last stitch p 1.
**8th row:** k 1, p 14, * k 2, p 14, repeat from * to last stitch, k 1.
**9th row:** * k 2 together, k 3, increase 1, k 6, increase 1, k 3, sl 1, k 1, psso, repeat from * to end.
**10th row:** Purl.
Repeat 1st to 10th rows till work measures 38cm from beginning.

**Shape for armhole**: Keeping continuity of pattern, cast off 8 *(14)* stitches at beginning of next 2 rows. Cast off 4 stitches at the beginning of the next 4 rows *(dec 1 st at beginning of the next 16 rows—132 sts)*.
Continue without shaping till work measures 61cm from beginning.

**Shape for shoulder**:
**1st and 2nd rows:** Work in pattern to last 10 stitches, turn.
**3rd and 4th rows:** Work in pattern to last 20 stitches, turn.
**5th and 6th rows:** Work in pattern to last 34 stitches, turn.
Work to end of row. Cast off.
*For the larger size, cast off 12 stitches at beginning of next 4 rows, then 15 stitches at beginning of next 2 rows. Cast off remaining stitches or, if you prefer, leave on a stitch holder.*

## FRONT

Work as for back till armhole shaping has been completed, then work 6 rows without shaping.

**Neck shaping**:
**Next row:** Work in pattern across 56 stitches, turn. *(K 2 tog, pattern 65 sts, K 2 tog, turn.)*
Decrease once at neck edge in next and every following 4th row till 54 stitches remain. Work without shaping till work measures same as back at armhole edge, and ending at neck edge. *(Decrease at neck edge every 4 rows, at same time decrease at armhole edge in alternate rows until 39 stitches remain.)*

**Shape for shoulder**:
**1st row:** Work to last 10 stitches, turn.
**2nd row:** Work to end.
**3rd row:** Work to last 20 stitches, turn.
**4th row:** Work to end. Cast off.
*(For larger size, cast off 12 stitches at beginning of next 2 rows, then cast off remaining 15 stitches.)*
Join in wool at neck edge, and work other side to correspond.

## NECKBAND

Sew up left shoulder.
Using 2mm needles, with right side of work facing, knit up 44 *(54)* stitches along back, 74 *(88)* stitches evenly along left front, 1 stitch in centre (mark this stitch with coloured wool), 74 *(88)* stitches evenly along right front.
**1st row:** k 1, * k 1, p 1, repeat from * to end.
**2nd row:** * k 1, p 1, repeat from * to 5 stitches at centre front of neck, p 2 together, k 1, p 2 together, rib to end.
**3rd row:** k 1, * k 1, p 1, repeat from * to 5 centre stitches, k 2 together, p 1, k 2 tog, rib to end.
Repeat 2nd and 3rd rows 5 times.
Cast off loosely in rib.

## ARMHOLE BANDS

Sew up right shoulder. Using 2.00mm needles, with right side of work showing, knit up 184 *(208)* stitches evenly around armhole.

**1st row:** k 2, * p 1, k 1, repeat from * to end.
Repeat 1st row 11 times.
Cast off in rib.

### TO MAKE UP

With a damp cloth and warm iron, press lightly.
Sew up side seams.
The finished pullover will give years of wear if carefully stored when winter ends. Make sure that the pullover is clean. Place it in a polythene bag (such as a drycleaner's bag) and squeeze out as much air as you can before sealing the bag. To keep insects away, use mothballs. Commercial mothballs contain an insecticide, but if you don't like the smell you can try natural alternatives such as cedar, lavender or rosemary. Don't put these in the bag with the pullover, but merely put them alongside.

# Clyde

Polo-necked pullover with a rugged appeal for the out-of-doors man who has an eye for style.

*The Australian Women's Weekly*, 25 March 1939.

**Materials:** 650g Cleckheaton Country 8 ply 100% pure new wool; pair 3.75mm needles; set of four 3.00mm needles.
**Measurements:** Length from top of shoulder, 62cm. Chest, 96.5cm. Length of sleeve seam, 53cm.
**Tension:** 24 stitches and 32 rows to 10cm.

## BACK

Using 3mm needles cast on 114 stitches. Work in rib of k 1, p 1, for 9cm (working 1st row into back of stitches). Change to 3.75mm needles.
**1st row:** K 6, * p 6, k 6, repeat from * to end.
**2nd row:** p 6, * k 6, p 6, repeat from * to end.
Repeat last 2 rows twice.
**7th row:** p 6, * k 6, p 6, repeat from * to end.
**8th row:** k 6, * p 6, k 6, repeat from * to end.
Repeat last 2 rows twice. These 12 rows complete 1 pattern.
Continue in pattern until work measures 39cm.

**Shape armholes:**
Cast off 8 stitches at the beginning of the next 2 rows. K 2 tog at each end of the next 4 rows, then every 2nd row 4 times. When armholes measure 20cm, shape shoulders by casting off 7 stitches at the beginning of the next 8 rows. Cast off.

## FRONT

Work the same as for back until armholes measure 13cm.
**Next row:** Work 37 stitches (leave on spare needle) cast off 8 stitches, work 37 stitches. Continue on last 37 stitches and k 2 tog at neck edge of the next 4 rows, then every 2nd row until decreased to 28 stitches. When armhole measures 20cm, shape shoulder by casting off 7 stitches at armhole edge every 2nd row, 4 times. Join wool and work other side to correspond.

Originally knitted in 'Sun-Glo' Shrinkproof 4 ply fingering wool, shade No. 347 (grey), we have updated it in a machine-washable 8 ply wool.

## SLEEVES

Using 3.00 needles cast on 66 stitches Work in rib of k 1, p 1 for 9cm (working 1st row into back of stitches). Change to 3.75mm needles and work in pattern, increasing 1 stitch each end of every 12th row until increased to 78 stitches then every 8th row until increased to 92 stitches. Work 8 rows. K 2 tog at each end of every row until decreased to 18 stitches. Cast off.

## NECK

Join shoulder seams. With right side of work towards you, using four 3.00mm needles, pick up and knit about 120 stitches around neck. Work in rib of k 1, p 1 for 11.5cm. Cast off loosely.

## TO MAKE UP

Press with a warm iron and damp cloth. Sew up seams, sew in sleeves, placing seam to seam.

# Knitting therapy

Research has found the practice of knitting to have substantial psychological and social benefits that can improve quality of life and overall wellbeing. Knitting can give people a feeling of accomplishment and sense of confidence as well as the satisfaction of creating something useful.

One international survey of 3,545 knitters found that people who knit more often felt calmer and happier. Another survey of more than 3,000 people found that knitting and crochet helped people relax, reduced their stress and improved their mood. Knitting has also been associated with decreased risk of cognitive impairment associated with ageing.

Knitting has also been found to help manage chronic pain, partly due to its rhythmic, repetitive movements. A study found that three-quarters of those living with health challenges reported that knitting and crochet helped them cope. Preliminary research also shows that knitting may be beneficial in the clinical management of specific anxieties.

Former bishop Richard Rutt resumed his childhood hobby of knitting as an adult. He wrote *A History of Hand Knitting*, in which he describes several cases of men who declared that their sanity and health had been saved by knitting. He quotes mid-twentieth-century Archbishop of Canterbury Geoffrey Fisher: 'Knitting is a distinct virtue. It's reflective and repetitive. Whenever you are engaged in doing a purely repetitive thing, your mind can reflect upon life'.

There are clear benefits to children in learning to knit. Knitting involves reading and following instructions, as well as arithmetic through counting stitches and rows and working out pattern repeats. At the Waldorf School in Chicago where all first graders learn to knit, teachers say it helps their reading as they follow the stitches across the fabric and see patterns forming. Knitting also helps develop fine motor skills and gives children practice in solving problems and fixing errors when something goes wrong. The rhythmic nature of knitting can be calming for children, and it allows them to express their creativity by choosing colours and patterns. The craft has a positive influence on children, giving them a sense of accomplishment, greater self-confidence, perseverance and better concentration.

# Ganseys, guernseys and jerseys

Traditional fishermen's ganseys (also known as guernseys or jerseys, after the English Channel islands on which they were made) are decorative, warm woollen sweaters favoured by sailors. The pattern on page 79 is a gansey-style jumper.

The stitch patterns that form the fabric of the ganseys developed differently in the various villages along the coasts of the British Isles and also in northern France and the Netherlands. It is said that it was possible to identify sailors by the distinctive patterns on their ganseys: the island or village from which he came and sometimes even his family was identified in the particular arrangement of cables and bobbles.

Unsurprisingly, the gansey stitch patterns are inspired by sailing and the sea. They represent ropes, ladders, waves, nets and sand, among other things. For many years the stitch patterns were passed down only through fishing families, but the proliferation of printed knitting patterns that became available from the middle of the twentieth century has now made them popular around the world.

ABOVE A gansey design with pigtail cables; RIGHT A gansey-clad man carries fishing gear on Melbourne's Sandringham beach circa 1955.

In the original magazine, 'this jersey is ideal for yachting, as Viyella wool is used—this wool is guaranteed unshrinkable, colour fast. And no matter how many dips it may have in the briny, the jersey will not sag or bag, will never lose its shape—so it's well worth the making'.

Our updated version is knitted in Bendigo Woollen Mills Classic 5 ply, a machine washable 100 % wool yarn. The colour is Napoleon Blue, an appropriately militaristic colour that is also reminiscent of the traditional dark blue seaman's guernseys of the Channel Islands (see page 77).

# Stuart

Of course, men like smart knitteds; that is why we chose this aristocrat among them. Any old kind of sweater, pullover, or jersey will not do the man of today. He likes comfort, oh, yes!—but he prefers that this quality or quantity is supplemented by 'good looks' in the clothes he wears.

*The Australian Women's Weekly*, 25 April 1936.

The pattern is distinctive and very neat, and the body is made with a snappy little diagonal rib with two lines of cable stitch on either side. The sleeves are worked in stocking stitch, the polo collar and cuffs in a k 2, p 2 rib.

**Materials:** 750g Bendigo Woollen Mills Classic 5 ply in Napoleon Blue; pair each of 3.25mm and 2.75mm needles; set of four 2.75mm double-pointed needles; one cable needle; 8 stitch markers.

**Measurements:** Length: 70cm; chest: 108cm; sleeve; 56cm.

**Tension:** 31 stitches and 36 rows to 10cm in pattern.

### FRONT

Cast on 136 sts loosely with 2.75mm needles. Rib k 2, p 2 for 9cm (29 rows). Change to 3.25mm needles. Knit 1 row increasing 1 stitch in the 1st and every 5th stitch to 164 stitches.

Purl 1 row putting in markers after 27, 8, 9, 8, 60, 8, 9, 8 stitches

**1st pattern row:** * K 1, k 2 tog, put the left needle through the back loop of the 2 stitches just knitted together (it will be found to be usually quite loose as the work proceeds), k into the loop *, repeat * to * 8 times, k 8, repeat pattern on next 9 stitches, k 8, pattern on 60, k 8, pattern on 9, k 8, pattern on 27.

**2nd pattern row:** Purl.

**3rd pattern row:** * K 2 tog, pick up back loop and k, k 1 * repeat 8 times. k 8, * k 2 tog, pick up back loop and k, k 1 * repeat twice, k 8, * k 2 tog, pick up back loop and k, k 1 * repeat 19 times, k 8, * k 2 tog, pick up back loop and k, k 1 * repeat twice, k 8 * k 2 tog, pick up back loop and k, k 1 * repeat 8 times.

**4th pattern row:** purl.

Repeat these 4 rows once.

The next row of pattern is also the cable row.

Twist the cables as follows: pattern on 27 stitches, slip the next 4 stitches onto the cable needle, and leave in front of work, k the next 4 stitches, then the 4 stitches from the cable needle. Pattern on 9 stitches, cable, pattern on 60, cable, pattern on 9, cable, pattern to end.

Work 1 row in p.

Repeat these 10 rows (pattern rows 1–4 twice, cable row, purl row) until the work measures 70cm from the beginning. Cast off 50 stitches loosely, transfer next 64 stitches to the 3.25mm DPNs, cast off 50 stitches loosely.

## BACK

Knit the back exactly the same as for the front and join the shoulders.

## POLO COLLAR

Arrange the 128 stitches for the neck on 3 needles, and rib k 2, p 2, for 9cm.

Cast off loosely.

## SLEEVES

Cast on 84 stitches with 2.75mm needles.

Rib k 2, p 2 for 10cm.

Change to 3.25mm needles, and knit in stocking stitch, increasing 1 stitch each end of every 8th row until work measures 46cm (not including cuff when pressed). Cast off loosely.

## TO MAKE UP

Press work lightly, and sew in the sleeves. Press seams. Sew up side and sleeve seams and press.

# Sheep breeds and their wool

Different breeds of sheep produce fleeces with characteristics that affect their suitability for spinning and garment making.

Sheep such as Border Leicester and Romney tend to produce heavy fleeces with long, coarse fibres. Their wool is favoured for handspinning due to its longer length.

Wool with very coarse fibres (often from northern European sheep breeds such as Scottish Blackface and Icelandic) is called carpet wool, used to make carpets and tapestries.

Medium-wool sheep (Southdown, Dorset, Suffolk) produce the lightest weight, least valuable fleeces. Medium wool is usually made into blankets, jumpers or socks or may be felted.

The fleeces with the greatest value come from fine-wool sheep (Merino, Rambouillet) and are prized for their versatility of use. Garments made from fine wool are the most comfortable against the skin and are less likely to itch.

Australia has three main types of sheep: merinos, British breeds and hybrids.

### Merinos

The Merino is Australia's major sheep breed and has made Australia famous for the quality of its wool (see page 23). The Merino produces a fine-wool fleece that is dense and short. It grows in small bundles and is usually bright white in colour. Its fine fibres have little twists that interlock in the spinning process, and the grease of the raw wool has antibacterial effects. The fleece can be spun using the woollen or worsted method, but can be difficult for inexperienced handspinners because of its softness, short fibres and stickiness.

Merino wool is the softest type of wool available and produces fine yarns for knitting and crochet.

LEFT Bales of fine merino wool at an auction yard in Sydney in about 2009; ABOVE Frank Hurley's heroic portrait of a Merino ram.

Fine merino is ideal for garments worn against the skin, baby clothes, shawls, and other fine knitwear, but it is not suitable for heavy jumpers or durable everyday garments. Fine merino wools blend well with other fibres such as cashmere, alpaca, angora, camel, silk, and mohair.

**British breeds**

British long-wool breeds include Lincoln, Cheviot, Border Leicester and Romney Marsh. They produce a long fleece that is easier for handspinners to work with. The wool is suited for medium to heavyweight fabrics. Lincoln wool is popular for use in rugs and wall hangings.

British short-wool breeds, commonly known as Downs breeds, grow wool that is comparatively harsh to handle and is flat in lustre. Downs breeds include Southdown, Dorset Horn, Ryeland, Dorset Down, Suffolk and Shropshire Down.

**Hybrids**

Australia's Merino sheep have been crossbred with British breeds to produce sheep that combine the high quality of the merino wool with other desirable characteristics, such as larger frames, heavier fleeces or longer fibres. Some of these sheep are now distinct breeds, such as the Corriedale and Polwarth, which produce fleeces popular with handspinners.

In the mid-twentieth century, crossbreed wool was promoted by textile company Patons as having superior durability, making it ideal for outdoor garments and hard-wearing apparel such as sportswear.

# William

Just what he needs now. Choose a good, practical colour and make it with or without sleeves. He'll appreciate a pullover like this for year-round wear.

*The Australian Women's Weekly*, 15 June 1940.

**Materials:** 750g Cleckheaton Country Naturals 8 ply in Oxblood; pair each of 3.75mm and 3.00mm needles and set of four 3.00mm double-pointed needles.
**Measurements:** To fit 92–96.5cm chest. Length from shoulder to hem, 51cm (our sample was knitted with an extra 10cm of length in the body). Sleeve seam, 51cm.
**Tension:** 24 stitches and 32 rows to 10cm.
**Note:** Work into back of all cast-on stitches.

## BACK

Cast on 120 stitches on 2 3.00mm needles. **
Work k 1, p 1 rib for 30 rows, k 2 tog at each end of last row (118 stitches).
Change to 3.75mm needles and pattern.
**1st and 3rd rows:** k 4, * p 2, k 4 *. Repeat * to * to end.
**2nd and 4th rows:** p 4, * k 2, p 4, *. Repeat * to * to end.
**5th row:** Purl.
**6th row:** Knit.
These 6 rows form the pattern.
Repeat the pattern 11 times or until desired length, then work first 4 rows of next pattern.
Work should measure 28cm from cast on.
**Shape armholes:** Cast off 6 stitches at beginning of next 2 rows.
K 2 tog at beginning of next 12 rows (94 stitches).**
Continue in pattern on 94 stitches until armholes measure 21.5cm, measured straight up.
**Shape shoulders:** Cast off 6 stitches at beginning of next 8 rows. Place remaining stitches on spare needle.

## FRONT

Cast on 120 stitches on 3.00mm needles.
Work exactly as given for back from ** to ** (94 stitches after armhole shaping).

You can make this pullover with long sleeves or without just as you prefer. For winter wear, we suggest long sleeves, but the same design without the sleeves could be used for making several pullovers for wearing at other times of the year.

The original yarn was Glenada Highland Mixtures, Shade J.5 (brown mixture); our updated version is knitted in Cleckheaton Country Naturals 8 ply in Oxblood with a lovely flecked finish.

**Divide for neck:** Pattern 45, k 2 together.
Work on these stitches only, placing the 47 stitches on spare needle.
*** Pattern 46.
K 2 tog at neck edge on every alternate row until 24 stitches remain.
Continue in pattern on 24 stitches until armhole measures 21.5cm, measured straight up, ending at armhole edge.
**Shape shoulder:** * Cast off 6 stitches, work to end.
Work wrong side row. *
Repeat * to * twice. Cast off ***.
Join yarn at centre to stitches left unworked and k 2 tog, pattern to end.
Work from *** to *** to match other shoulder.

## SLEEVES (BOTH ALIKE)

Cast on 64 stitches on 3.00mm needles. Work k 1, p 1 rib for 30 rows. Change to 3.75mm needles and pattern. Work the 6 pattern rows twice.
Continue in pattern, increasing 1 stitch at each end of next and every 10th row until 84 stitches are on needle, working increased stitches into pattern.
Increase 1 stitch at each end of every 8th row until 94 stitches are on needle.
Continue on 94 stitches until work measures 51cm from cast on.
Cast off 3 stitches at beginning of next 2 rows.
Knit 2 together at beginning of every row until 64 stitches remain.
K 2 tog at each end of every row until 36 stitches remain. Cast off, knitting 2 together at each end.

### NECK RIBBING

Sew up shoulder seams. With right side of work facing, commence at left shoulder, using four 3.00mm double-pointed needles pick up and k 68 stitches to centre front, 68 stitches to right shoulder and 46 back stitches (182 stitches total).

Working round and round in k 1, p 1 rib, k 2 tog each side of centre front for 8 rows. Cast off in rib, using a 3.75mm needle to ensure looseness, knitting 2 together each side of centre front as before.

### TO MAKE UP

Press work on wrong side with hot iron over damp cloth. Sew up side and sleeve seams. Sew sleeves into armholes.

**Sleeveless:** Using the four 3.00mm double-pointed needles, pick up and k stitches round armholes. Work k 1, p 1 rib for 8 rows. Cast off in rib, using a 3.75mm needle.

Press all seams.

The original of this sportsman's sweater was knitted in Lincoln Mills 'Daphne' crochet wool. We've updated it with 5 ply machine washable wool yarn in sporting white.

# Robert

Here is the right sweater for the cricketer, golfer and tennis player, plus a substantial and cosy scarf to slip on when play is over.

*The Australian Women's Weekly*, 4 August 1954.

**Materials:** 600g Bendigo Woollen Mills Classic 5 ply 100% wool yarn; set of four 2.75mm needles; pair each 3.75mm and 3.00mm needles; 1 cable needle.
**Measurements:** To fit 92–96.5cm chest. Length from shoulder, 61cm. Length of sleeve, 55.5cm.
**Cable:** To 'twist' cable, slip the next three stitches on to the cable needle and place at back of work, knit the next three stitches, then knit the three stitches on the cable needle.

## BACK

Cast on 136 stitches on 3.00mm needles, knit in single (k 1, p 1) rib for 7.5cm. Cast on 1 stitch. Change to 3.75mm needles and knit as follows:
**1st row:** P 2, *k 1, p 1, k 1, p 2, k 2, p 2, k 2, p 2, repeat from * until 5 stitches remain, k 1, p 1, k 1, p 2.
**2nd row:** K 2, * p 3, k 2, p 2, k 2, p 2, k 2, repeat from * until 5 stitches remain, p 3, k 2.
Repeat these two rows twice more.
**7th row:** p 2, * k 1, p 1, k 1, p 2, cable, p 2, repeat from * until 5 stitches remain, k 1, p 1, k 1, p 2.
**8th row:** k 2, * p 3, k 2, p 6, k 2, repeat from * until 5 stitches remain, p 3, k 2.
**9th and 10th rows:** As 1st and 2nd rows.
These 10 rows complete the pattern.
Repeat pattern 10 times more; this brings you to the armhole.
**Shape armholes:** Cast off 9 stitches at the beginning of the next 2 rows, then decrease 1 stitch at each end of every 2nd row 5 times. Continue in pattern until armhole measures 28cm.
**Shape shoulders:** Cast off 8 stitches at the beginning of the next 8 rows. Cast off remainder.

## FRONT

Knit exactly as for the back until 10 patterns are completed, then knit 4 more rows.

**Shape neck:** Knit in pattern for 67 stitches, then k 2 tog. With another ball of wool knit remainder of row. Continue knitting this way and decrease 1 stitch at neck ends of the next and every 4th row to follow. At the same time, when the 11th pattern is completed, shape armholes as for back. Knit until you have 32 stitches on each side of front.

**Shape shoulders:** Cast off 8 stitches at armhole ends 4 times.

### SLEEVES

Cast on 70 stitches on 3.00mm needles. Knit in single rib for 7.5cm. Cast on 1 stitch at each end of the last row of rib (72 stitches). Change to 3.75mm needles. Knit in pattern as for back, increase 1 stitch at each end of every 10th row until 14 patterns are completed (98 stitches). Work one more pattern without shaping.

**Shape armhole:** Cast off 9 stitches at beginning of next two rows, then decrease 1 stitch at each end of every 4th row until there are 58 stitches, then decrease each end of every 2nd row until there are 48 stitches. Cast off.

### NECK BAND

First join shoulder seams. With the four 3.00mm needles, pick up stitches around the neck and knit in single rib for 9 rows (71 stitches on each side of neck plus cast-off stitches across top of back). Cast off.

### TO MAKE UP

Press all parts on wrong side with hot iron over a damp cloth. Sew side seams and insert sleeves.

## SCARF

**Materials:** 250g Bendigo Woollen Mills Classic 5 ply 100% wool yarn. 1 pair of 5.5mm knitting needles.

Cast on 70 stitches and work in ribbing of k 2, p 2 throughout for 136cm or length required.

**To make fringe:** Wind wool around fingers three times—break off and use a crochet hook to draw a loop through the border row of the scarf—pass the ends through the loop and draw up firmly. Repeat evenly along both ends of the scarf.

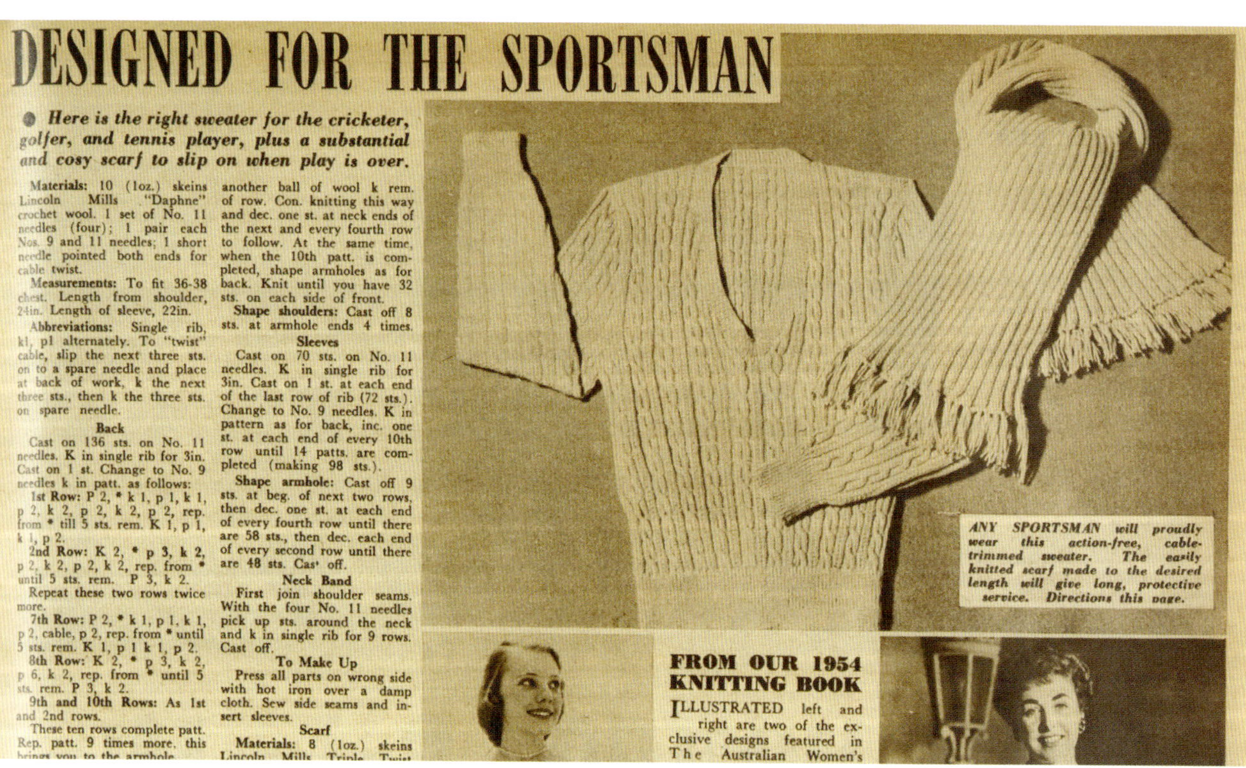

# DESIGNED FOR THE SPORTSMAN

*Here is the right sweater for the cricketer, golfer, and tennis player, plus a substantial and cosy scarf to slip on when play is over.*

**Materials:** 10 (1oz.) skeins Lincoln Mills "Daphne" crochet wool. 1 set of No. 11 needles (four); 1 pair each Nos. 9 and 11 needles; 1 short needle pointed both ends for cable twist.

**Measurements:** To fit 36-38 chest. Length from shoulder, 24in. Length of sleeve, 22in.

**Abbreviations:** Single rib, k1, p1 alternately. To "twist" cable, slip the next three sts. on to a spare needle and place at back of work, k the next three sts., then k the three sts. on spare needle.

**Back**

Cast on 136 sts. on No. 11 needles. K in single rib for 3in. Cast on 1 st. Change to No. 9 needles k in patt. as follows:

**1st Row:** P 2, * k 1, p 1, k 1, p 2, k 2, p 2, k 2, p 2, rep. from * till 5 sts. rem. K 1, p 1, k 1, p 2.

**2nd Row:** K 2, * p 3, k 2, p 2, k 2, p 2, k 2, rep. from * until 5 sts. rem. P 3, k 2.

Repeat these two rows twice more.

**7th Row:** P 2, * k 1, p 1, k 1, p 2, cable, p 2, rep. from * until 5 sts. rem. K 1, p 1 k 1, p 2.

**8th Row:** K 2, * p 3, k 2, p 6, k 2, rep. from * until 5 sts. rem. P 3, k 2.

**9th and 10th Rows:** As 1st and 2nd rows.

These ten rows complete patt. Rep. patt. 9 times more, this brings you to the armhole ...

another ball of wool k rem. of row. Con. knitting this way and dec. one st. at neck ends of the next and every fourth row to follow. At the same time, when the 10th patt. is completed, shape armholes as for back. Knit until you have 32 sts. on each side of front.

**Shape shoulders:** Cast off 8 sts. at armhole ends 4 times.

**Sleeves**

Cast on 70 sts. on No. 11 needles. K in single rib for 3in. Cast on 1 st. at each end of the last row of rib (72 sts.). Change to No. 9 needles. K in pattern as for back, inc. one st. at each end of every 10th row until 14 patts. are completed (making 98 sts.).

**Shape armhole:** Cast off 9 sts. at beg. of next two rows, then dec. one st. at each end of every fourth row until there are 58 sts., then dec. each end of every second row until there are 48 sts. Cas' off.

**Neck Band**

First join shoulder seams. With the four No. 11 needles pick up sts. around the neck and k in single rib for 9 rows. Cast off.

**To Make Up**

Press all parts on wrong side with hot iron over a damp cloth. Sew side seams and insert sleeves.

**Scarf**

**Materials:** 8 (1oz.) skeins Lincoln Mills Triple Twist ...

*ANY SPORTSMAN will proudly wear this action-free, cable-trimmed sweater. The easily knitted scarf made to the desired length will give long, protective service. Directions this page.*

**FROM OUR 1954 KNITTING BOOK**

ILLUSTRATED left and right are two of the exclusive designs featured in The Australian Women's ...

# Breaking records

According to Guinness World Records, the world's fastest handknitter is Miriam Tegels of the Netherlands, who set a record in 2006 of 118 stitches in one minute.

Shearer Trevor Pike in action for The Spinning Knitwits during the Back to Back Wool Challenge in the Hunter Valley, 2008.

In 2004, Linda Benne set the North American speed-knitting record with a speed of 253 stitches in three minutes: that is one-and-a-half stitches per second. In 2008, Hazel Tindall of Shetland, UK, knitted 262 stitches in three minutes.

A record for the most people knitting together was set in September 2012 at the Royal Albert Hall, London, when 3,083 people knitted simultaneously for 15 minutes. In 1811, two men in England made a bet about whether a coat could be made from scratch in one day; that is, shearing the sheep, spinning the wool, weaving and dyeing the cloth, and then making the coat. The coat was finished in 13 hours and 20 minutes and worn at a dinner that same night. Today that challenge has become the International Back to Back Wool Challenge, for a team of eight (one shearer and seven spinners and knitters) to hand shear a sheep, spin the wool and knit a sweater within eight hours. In 2004, the Pembroke Merriwa Jumbucks from New South Wales' Hunter Valley set a world record of five hours and 51 minutes. As part of the same challenge, the Kurrajong team from New South Wales' Blue Mountains raised a total of $50,000 for the Cancer Council in the years 2007–2012.

# Children

Knitting for children can be fun: the small size of the garments makes for a quick knit, and you can be adventurous when it comes to colour and pattern. Knitted clothing is great for children because it is flexible and comfortable for them to wear in all kinds of situations, and the absorbent and elastic properties of woollen yarns mean the garments are hard-wearing and long-lasting too.

Modern yarns (whether woollen, wool blend, or other natural and synthetic fibres) have largely done away with the common complaint from children that knitwear is 'too scratchy'. So mothers and fathers, aunts and uncles can feel free to knit for the kids in their lives. Updating the patterns with modern yarns and colours makes the garments even more appealing.

At the time that these knitting patterns were first published in the 1930s and 40s, it was still considered appropriate to dress children in smaller versions of adult clothing. The knits presented here are quite structured and tailored compared to today's childrenswear. The Lorraine dress on page 102, for example, or the Fredrick vest on page 116, seem designed for more formal occasions, although they would have been considered perfectly acceptable play clothes at the time of publication.

One skein of wool makes this cosy baby's jacket

# Lynette

This slip-on jacket is so nice. It weighs very little, but will keep your cherub cosy.

*The Australian Women's Weekly*, 13 May 1944.

**Materials:** 60g Shepherd Baby Wool Merino (100% merino wool) or Patons Big Baby (60% acrylic, 40% nylon), 3 ply. 1 pair 3.00mm needles or 3.00mm circular needles. 1 metre narrow ribbon or crochet cord.
**Measurements:** 25cm (neck to hip); 52cm (under arms); 13cm (underarm to end sleeve).
**Tension:** 30 stitches and 40 rows to 10cm.
**Moss stitch:** K 1, p 1, repeat to end; turn and knit into the knit stitches of the previous row, purl into purl stitches of the previous row.

**Cast on 56 stitches** and knit 2 rows in moss stitch.
**3rd row:** Knit 3 stitches in moss stitch, then k 2 tog, and make 1 stitch by looping wool over needle. Continue k 2 tog and make 1 until 3 stitches remain. K 3 in moss stitch.
**4th and 5th rows:** Moss stitch.
**6th row:** K 5 moss stitch, then k 10,* wool forward, k 1, wool forward, k 1, wool forward, k 1, wool forward,* k 20. Repeat * to *, then k 10 and moss 5.
**7th row:** Moss stitch 5, purl to last 5, and then moss stitch 5. Keep 5 stitches in moss stitch at both ends of needle throughout the work.
**8 th row:** Moss stitch 5, then k 11, * wool forward, k 1. wool forward, k 3, wool forward, k 1, wool forward, * k 22. Repeat * to *, then k 11 and moss stitch 5.
**9th row:** Same as 7th.
**10th row:** Moss stitch 5, k 12, * wool forward,

k 1, wool forward, k 5, wool forward, k 1, wool forward, * k 24. Repeat * to *, then k 12 and moss stitch 5.

Continue increases in this manner until there are 25 rows of holes. *

**To make each sleeve**, slip stitches between holes on to a stitch holder and leave until later.

Continue knitting in stocking stitch, keeping the 5 moss stitches at the ends, until the work measures 23cm.

Knit 5 rows in moss stitch and cast off loosely.

Pick up sleeve stitches from the stitch holder and knit to required length.

Then knit 5 rows moss stitch and cast off.

**Sew up** sleeves, and thread ribbon or cord round the holes at neckline.

Baby wool is traditionally 3 or 4 ply pure new wool in white or pale pastel shades. To make it softer for baby's delicate skin, many manufacturers make baby yarns in acrylic, which also retains its shape better when washed (something that is frequently necessary with a baby's garments). These days, baby yarns are often available in many colours other than pastel pink, blue, yellow and white. The garment is knitted from the top down.

# Knitting for a cause

Knitting garments by hand to donate to a cause is common among knitters and knitting groups. Many charity organisations seek handknitted goods to distribute to people in need. Items most often sought include beanies and caps, bootees, socks, sweaters, scarves, gloves, blankets and rugs (or squares to make them), soft toys and teddy bears. Donated items may go to struggling families, people experiencing financial stress or homelessness, at-risk children, Indigenous communities, refugees, women's shelters and many more. Some donated items are sent overseas to people fleeing war or persecution, or experiencing disasters such as earthquake or floods. Donated items are also sold to raise funds for charities; for example, through charity shops.

Knitted items are not only donated to keep people warm. Red Cross Australia coordinates the collection and distribution of Trauma Teddies® made by volunteer knitters. The teddies are provided to services such as police, firefighters and emergency services to be given to anyone experiencing trauma and suffering, for example after a fire or road accident. The teddies can provide comfort and help to take people's minds off their plight. The teddies are knitted to a Red Cross pattern and every Trauma Teddy must pass a strict quality inspection before distribution.

Sometimes knitted items are used to raise awareness of a cause. The Little Yellow Duck Project is a global initiative that has been running since 2014. It raises awareness of the need for people to become organ, stem cell and blood donors. Volunteers knit or craft little yellow ducks to leave in public places for strangers to find. Each duck has a tag that invites the finder to take the duck home and to register on the project's website the place where the duck was found. The website provides information about the project and encourages the finder to register to become an organ donor.

Animals benefit from donated knitting items also. Animal rescue organisations need coats, blankets and pouches for animals that have been injured or orphaned, whether through bushfires, road accidents, barbed wire or illegal traps. One shelter uses small knitted blankets for wrapping baby animals or making into pouches for joeys. The blankets must be pure wool so the animals can breathe through the fabric as they snuggle underneath to minimise heat loss from their heads. They also must be machine washable as the baby animals are not toilet trained! During the drought of 2018, a shortage of feed led to starving ewes rejecting their newborn lambs in order to meet their own survival needs, and lambs being lost to the winter cold. A campaign to knit lamb jumpers was started to help the affected farmers. Patterns were shared via social networking websites, and knitters were connected with farmers whose lambs needed warm jumpers.

Some not-for-profit organisations have been established specifically to donate knitted goods to those in need. Wrap with Love, based in Sydney, accepts knitted or crocheted squares or blankets to keep people in need warm. Over 23 years, Wrap with Love has sent more than 400,000 blankets to people in more than 75 countries, including Australia. Knit One, Give One (KOGO) is a Victorian organisation that distributes warm

Red Cross Trauma Teddies®
are a good way to use up the
ends of balls of wool.

winter woollies knitted by volunteers to more than 250 community groups for people in need. Knit4Charities is an Australian internet-based network with members from across the world. It provides volunteers with patterns and ideas for knitting warm clothing, blankets and toys for a range of charities. Regular local meetings, called Knit and Natters, enable volunteers to share support and friendship as they knit.

Australia's state-based knitting guilds and organisations knit for a range of charities, and provide members with contact details of charities and their needs. In addition, many smaller groups and individuals knit for a cause, some for specific charities or causes such as asylum seekers in detention, refugees or women's refuges.

Knitting for charity is a good way to use up leftover yarn from larger projects, as many of the items are small projects such as beanies, scarves and toys. (In the case of blankets, you can knit small squares that can be sewn together to make larger rugs.) For those who enjoy knitting, but have run out of family members to outfit in woollies, it can be a way of indulging in a favourite hobby with a purpose. Do check with the charity you intend to knit for before you begin: some, like the Red Cross, have rules about what they will accept, while others can find themselves temporarily overwhelmed with more items than they can use or distribute, as was the case with the penguin colony on Phillip Island after a 2015 news story about Australia's oldest knitter, 109-year-old Alfie Date, inspired an influx of tiny penguin sweaters. They received so many sweaters that they will no longer accept new ones and will not need to for many years to come!

- redcross.org.au (search for trauma teddy)
- thelittleyellowduckproject.org
- facebook.com/lambjumpershelpingourfarmers
- wrapwithlove.org
- kogo.org.au
- knittersguildnsw.org.au/charity
- facebook.com/knittingforrefugees
- wires.org.au

Angora wool trims this little pullover

# Pamela

A simple jumper with a soft angora neckline, suitable for a six- to eight-year old.

*Country Life Knitting Book: A Variety of Garments for Babies and Children,* 1940s.

**Materials:** 400g Bendigo Woollen Mills Luxury 4 ply 100% wool; 10g Katia Pure Angora yarn. 1 pair each of 3.00mm and 2.75mm needles. 1 set of four 2.75mm double-pointed needles (DPNs).
**Measurements:** 66cm chest; 30.5cm sleeve seam.
**Tension:** 26 stitches and 35 rows to 10cm.

### FRONT

**Cast on** 84 stitches
**1st row:** K into back of every stitch.
**2nd row:** Rib k 2, p 2. Repeat for 10 rows rib, then start pattern of only 2 rows.
**1st row:** Knit.
**2nd row:** K 1, p 1.
Repeat these 2 rows until 20cm of pattern has been completed. Start armhole, cast off 4 stitches at beginning of each row for 4 rows then 2 at beginning of 5 rows. After 32 rows have been done from beginning of armhole, k 18 stitches, cast off 22 for neck, continue remaining stitches for 16 rows of shoulder, then cast off 4 stitches each row from armhole side of shoulder and 6 in the last row.
Join wool to other 18 stitches on needle and knit to correspond with first shoulder.

### BACK

Cast on 84 stitches, rib and knit the same as the front for 20cm of pattern, cast off for armhole, knit 44 rows and start to cast off for shoulder, 4 each row from armhole side of work 6 times, cast off remaining stitches for neck.

## SLEEVES

The sleeves are knitted from the top down. Cast on 24 stitches, start pattern and increase 1 stitch at beginning and end of every row until there are 64 stitches, continue for 6 rows and then decrease 1 stitch at beginning and end of every 6th row 4 times. When the sleeve measures 38cm from top change to 2.75mm DPNs and rib (k 2, p 2) for 7.5cm. Cast off.
Make another sleeve to match.

## TO MAKE UP

Press knitting with damp cloth and sew together. For neck, pick up 100 stitches on DPNs with angora wool. Rib (k 1, p 1) for 10 rows, k 2 tog at corners in front of the last 6 rows to draw in neck. Cast off.

# Angora Wool Trims this Little Girl's Pull-Over

## ...to fit 8-Year-old Child

THIS jumper is made with 5 ozs. of 4 ply Viyella Wool; ¼ oz. Angora wool; 2 No. 10 needles and 4 steel needles No. 12.

Cast on 84 sts.

**1st row.**—K into back of every st.

**2nd row.**—Rib k 2, p 2.

Repeat for 10 rows, then start pattern of only 2 rows.

**1st row.**—K.

**2nd row.**—K 1, p 1.

Repeat these 2 rows until 8 inches of pattern have been completed. Start armhole, cast off 4 sts at beginning of each row for 4 rows then 2 at beginning of 5 rows. After 32 rows have been done from beginning of armhole, k 18 sts, cast off 22 for neck, continue remaining sts for 16 rows of shoulder, then cast off 4 sts each row from armhole side of shoulder and 6 in the last row. Join wool to other 18 sts on needle and k to correspond with first shoulder.

BACK

Cast on 84 sts, rib and k the same as the front for 8 inches of pattern, cast off for armhole, k 44 rows and start to cast off for shoulder 4 each row from armhole side of work 6 times, cast off remaining sts for neck.

SLEEVE

Cast on 24 sts, start pattern and make 1 at beginning and end of every row until there are 64 sts, continue 6 rows and then dec 1 st at beginning and end of every 6th row 4 times. When the sleeve measures 15 inches from top change to steel needles and rib (k 2, p 2) for 3 inches, cast off.

Press knitting with damp cloth and machine together. For neck pick up 102 sts on 4 steel needles, with Angora wool, rib (k 1, p 1) for 10 rows, k 2 tog at corners in front of the last 4 rows to draw in neck. Cast off.

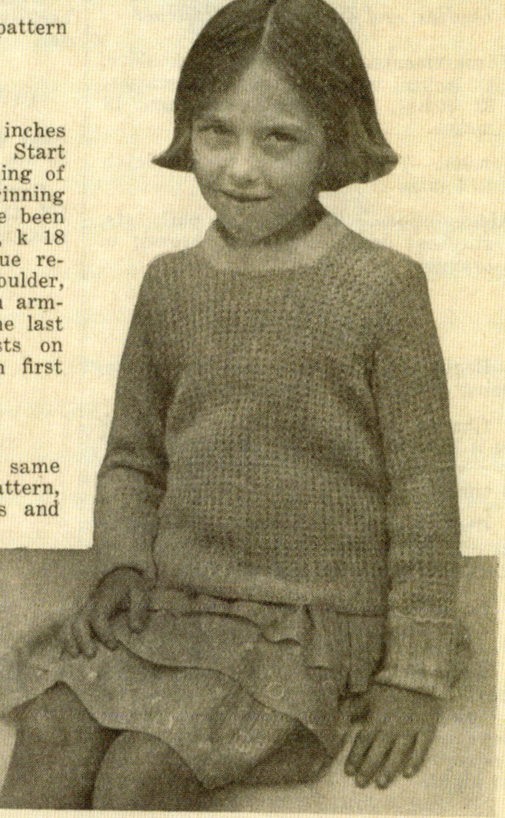

*Another cosy pull-over that is smart as well as very warm.*

*A little pull-over for the four to six year old boy. The model is in 4-ply heather wool.*

# DONALD PULL-OVER IS COSY

•

*MATERIALS.—4 skeins 4 ply heather wool; 1 pair Nos. 9 and 12 needles.*

**Measurements.**—Length from shoulder to lower edge, 14 inches; width all round underarms, 24 inches; length of sleeve from underarm, 11 inches.

Commence at lower edge of back by casting on 80 sts. K in ribbing of 2 plain, 2 purl for 2½ inches. Change to No. 9 needles.

Change to stocking st and continue until work measures 10 inches. Cast off 10 sts at beginning of next 2 rows for armholes and continue without shaping until work measures 13½ inches.

K 18 sts, cast off 24 sts, k remaining 18 sts, put first 18 sts on spare needle and continue on one shoulder for half an inch. Cast off, make other side to correspond.

FRONT

Follow directions as for back until 1 inch past armholes, shape as follows: K 29 sts, cast off 2 sts, k remaining 29 sts; put first 29 sts on spare needle and continue on one side, dec once on every alternate row at neck edge only, until work measures 14 inches and you have 18 sts left. Cast off.

Make other side to correspond.

SLEEVES

Cast on 48 sts on No. 12 needles and k in ribbing of 2 plain, 2 purl for 2½ inches.

Change to stocking stitch and No. 9 needles and inc once at each end of every 4th row until sleeve measures 11 inches and you have 64 sts. Cast off 3 sts at beginning of every row until sleeve measures 13 inches. Cast off.

Pick up sts at neck on fine sock needles and k 4 rows of 1 plain 1 purl. Cast off.

Join up and sew in sleeves, press under damp cloth.

### Stocking Stitch

*STOCKING STITCH is plain knitting, round and round on four needles. If you use two needles, knit a row then turn and purl back to produce the same result.*

Charming frock for a little girl

# Lorraine

Designed for a child of five to six years, just the prettiest thing for afternoon wear, and even for winter parties.

*The Australian Women's Weekly*, 8 May 1937.

**Materials:** 300g Heirloom 3 ply Baby Merino wool. 3.00mm needles.
**Measurements:** Shoulder to hem, 55cm, chest about 68cm, sleeve at underarm seam 11cm.
**Tension:** 32 stitches and 40 rows to 10cm.

## FRONT

Cast on 155 stitches.
**Moss stitch border:**
**1st row:** *k 1, p 1, repeat from * to last st, k 1.
Repeat 1st row 7 times (8 rows).
**Diamond pattern:**
**Row 1:** (9th row of garment) k 1, * yrn, ssk, k 17, k 2 tog, yrn, k 1, repeat from * to end of row.
**Row 2 and every even row:** k 1, p to last st, k 1.
**Row 3:** k 2, * yrn, ssk, k 15, k 2 tog, yrn, k 3, repeat from * to last 21 stitches, yrn, ssk, k 15, k 2 tog, yrn, k 2.
**Row 5:** k 3, *yrn, ssk, k 13, k 2 tog, yrn, k 5, repeat from * to last 20 stitches, yrn, ssk, k 13, k 2 tog, yrn, k 3.
**Row 7:** k 4, *yrn, ssk, k 11, k 2 tog, yrn, k 7, repeat from * to last 19 stitches, yrn, ssk, k 11, k 2 tog, yrn, k 4.
**Row 9:** k 5, *yrn, ssk, k 9, k 2 tog, yrn, k 9, repeat from * to last 18 stitches, yrn, ssk, k9, k 2 tog, yrn, k 5.
**Row 11:** k 6, *yrn, ssk, k7, k 2 tog, yrn, k 11, repeat from * to last 17 stitches, yrn, ssk, k 7, k 2 tog, yrn, k 6.
**Row 13:** k 7, *yrn, ssk, k 5, k 2 tog, yrn, k 13, repeat from * to last 16 stitches, yrn, ssk, k 5, k 2 tog, yrn, k 7.
**Row 15:** k 8, *yrn, ssk, k 3, k 2 tog, yrn, k 15, repeat from * to last 15 stitches, yrn, ssk, k 3, k 2 tog, yrn, k 8.
**Row 17:** k 9, *yrn, ssk, k 1, k 2 tog, yrn, k 17, repeat from * to last 14 stitches, yrn, ssk, k 1, k 2 tog, yrn, k 9.
**Row 19:** k 10, *yrn, (sl 1, k 2 tog, psso), yrn, k 19, repeat from * to last 13 stitches, yrn,

The original model was made in Lincoln Mills 'Waratah' crepe wool in a dainty blue shade; we updated it with Heirloom 3 ply Baby Merino premium machine washable wool.

(sl 1, k 2 tog, psso), yrn, k 10.
**Row 21:** k 9, *k 2 tog, yrn, k 1, yrn, ssk, k 17, repeat from * to last 14 stitches, k 2 tog, yrn, k 1, yrn, ssk, k 9.
**Row 23:** k 8, *k 2 tog, yrn, k 3, yrn, ssk, k 15, repeat from * to last 15 stitches, k 2 tog, yrn, k 3, yrn, ssk, k 8.
**Row 25:** k 7, * k 2 tog, yrn, k 5, yrn, ssk, k 13, repeat from * to last 16sts, k 2 tog, yrn, k 5, yrn, ssk, k 7.
**Row 27:** k 6, * k 2 tog, yrn, k 7, yrn, ssk, k 11, repeat from * to last 17sts, k 2 tog, yrn, k 7, yrn, ssk, k 6.
**Row 29:** k 5, * k 2 tog, yrn, k 9, yrn, ssk, k 9, repeat from * to last 18sts, k 2 tog, yrn, k 9, yrn, ssk, k 5.
**Row 31:** k 4, *k 2 tog, yrn, k 11, yrn, ssk, k 7, repeat from * to last 19sts, k 2 tog, yrn, k 11, yrn, ssk, k 4.
**Row 33: k 3**, *k 2 tog, yrn, k 13, yrn, ssk, k 5, repeat from * to last 20sts, k 2 tog, yrn, k 13, yrn, ssk, k 3.
**Row 35:** k 2, *k 2 tog, yrn, k 15, yrn, ssk, k 3, repeat from * to last 21sts, k 2 tog, yrn, k 15, yrn, ssk, k 2.
**Row 37:** k 1, *k 2 tog, yrn, k 17, yrn, ssk, k 1, repeat from * to last 22sts, k 2 tog, yrn, k 17, yrn, ssk, k 1.
**Row 39:** k 2 tog, *yrn, k 19, yrn, (sl1, k 2 tog, psso), repeat from * to last 21sts, yrn, k 19, yrn, ssk
**Row 40:** k 1, p to last stitch, k 1.
Repeat these 40 rows, decreasing 1 stitch at each end of 9th row and every following 5th row until 111 stitches remain and the work measures 40cm. Continue working in pattern to row 20 (or row 40 if longer skirt is required).

**Yoke:**
The yoke is worked in the same pattern (moss stitch) as the lower border of the dress, shape the armholes.
Cast off 3 stitches at the beginning of the next 6 rows (93 stitches).

Decrease 1 stitch each end of the needle in the next 5 rows (83 stitches).
Work until armhole measures 11cm.
In the next row, pattern 25 stitches, cast off the 33 centre stitches, pattern 25 stitches and finish the front in two parts.
Knit in pattern for 21 rows of right front.
**Shape shoulder:** At the neck edge, work 9 stitches, turn, work back to neck edge, work 17 stitches, turn, work back to neck edge, cast off all 25 stitches.
Join wool at neck edge of left front, and knit 20 rows in pattern.
Shape the other shoulder to match.

## BACK

Work as for front until armhole shaping in yoke is completed (83 stitches). Continue moss stitch pattern on these 83 stitches until work measures 11.5cm (62 rows).
**Next row:** Pattern 28 stitches, cast off 27 stitches in the centre for the neck, pattern 28 stitches and finish the back in two parts.
Cast off 1 stitch at the neck edge of the next 3 rows, while shaping the shoulder as for the front.
Shape the other shoulder to match.

## SLEEVES

Commence at the lower edge by casting on 49 stitches and work the cuff in border pattern for 6 rows, then:
**1st row:** k 2, *yrn, ssk, k 17, k 2 tog, yrn, k 1, repeat from * to end of row, k 1.
**2nd row:** k 1, p to last stitch, k 1.
Continue in diamond pattern as placed in previous two rows. Increase 1 stitch each side of the sleeve every second row until there are 85 stitches.
When sleeve measures 11cm, cast off 2 stitches at the beginning of the next 6 rows, then decrease 1 stitch at the beginning of every row until 41 stitches remain. Cast off.

## COLLAR

It consists of three sections, and is knitted in eyelet pattern, as follows:
With wrong side of front facing you, pick up 33 stitches.
**1st row:** Purl.
**2nd row:** k 1, *yrn, k 2 tog, repeat from * to end of row.
**3rd row:** Purl.
**4th row:** *ssk, yrn, repeat from * to last stitch, k 1.
Repeat these 2 rows for 5cm. Cast off in rib.
Pick up 21 stitches at side of neck and knit in the same way. Repeat on other side of neck.

## TO MAKE UP

Press all pieces with a hot iron over a damp cloth, sew up side, shoulder, and sleeve seams.
Sew sleeves in, seam to seam, pleating the upper part.

# Purling in protest

Knitting as a form of protest goes back to the French Revolution, when 'les Tricoteuses' (from the word *tricoter*, to knit) knitted in the Place de la Revolution while watching executions at the guillotine. These women knitted in protest against the revolutionary government's 1793 decision to exclude women from active participation in political assembly. This government was nervous about the power of women, following the huge success of the 1789 women's march on Versailles protesting against chronic food shortages and high prices. Les Tricoteuses knitted stockings and mittens, but also hundreds of red Phrygian caps or 'Liberty Caps' which came to symbolise the revolutionary values of liberty, equality and fraternity.

Like les Tricoteuses, people still gather to knit in public as a form of protest. In 2008, women set up chairs and knitted opposite the gate to the Aldermaston Atomic Weapons Establishment, Britain's nuclear bomb factory, to protest against nuclear weapons.

Knitting Nannas Against Gas was established in 2012 in the Northern Rivers area of New South Wales in response to the increasing exploration for coal seam gas in prime agricultural land. They describe themselves as an 'international disorganisation' of people who come together to preserve the environment for future generations. They continue the history of knitting for peaceful activism. The Knitting Nannas knit in yellow and black to reflect the 'Lock the Gate' triangles mounted at entrances to properties. They knit functional items as well as symbolic objects: long knitted banners to string across gates and access roads, as well as cushions and 'chain sleeves' for protesters locked to objects. In 2016, three members of the Knitting Nannas were arrested after they chained themselves by their necks to the gate of a wastewater plant near Narrabri, New South Wales. The Knitting Nannas have an extensive national and international membership, supported by a website, Facebook and Twitter.

Internationally, in recent years the 'Pussyhat™', a pink knitted beanie with pointed cat ears, has become a symbol of female empowerment and solidarity for women's rights. The movement to raise awareness of women's issues and create social change began the day after the inauguration of Donald Trump as the 45th President of the United States, when more than 600 women's solidarity marches took place across the US and across the world, including the Women's March on Washington, D.C.

A French woman knits red stockings as troops of the revolutionary army depart for the front.

Three-ply fingering wool was replaced with 3 ply Baby Wool. This will fit approximately a one-year old, either boy or girl.

# Beverly

Knitted in any shade, this delightful twin-set will look the tops. The right choice for a toddler's high days and holidays. The pattern is a fancy rib. The jumper has a garter-stitch band round the neck, and the little cardigan is edged with garter stitch.

*Australian Home Journal*, 1 April 1950.

**Materials:** 200g Shepherd Baby Wool Merino 3 ply; 1 pair of 3.00mm knitting needles; 3.00mm crochet hook; 6 small buttons.
**Measurements:** Cardigan: Length from shoulder, 25.5cm; width all round under the arms, 53cm; length of sleeve seam, 23cm.
**Jumper:** Length from shoulder, 24cm; width all round under the arms, 51cm; sleeve seam, 7.5cm.
**Tension:** 35 stitches and 48 rows to 10cm.

## CARDIGAN

### BACK

Cast on 86 stitches and work in pattern as follows:
**1st row:** K 1, * k 1, p 2, k 1, p 1; rep from * to end.
**2nd row:** Purl.
These 2 rows form the pattern. Continue to repeat them until work measures 15cm from beginning, ending with a purl row.

**Armhole shaping:** Cast off 4 stitches at beginning of next 2 rows, cast off 2 stitches at beginning of next 2 rows, then decrease 1 stitch at beginning of next 2 rows. Continue without shaping until work measures 25.5cm from beginning, ending with a purl row.
**Shoulder shaping:** Cast off 10 stitches at beginning of next 4 rows. Cast off remainder.

### RIGHT FRONT

Cast on 49 stitches.
**1st row:** K 6, * k 1, p 1, k 1, p 2, rep from * to last 3 stitches, k 1, p 1, k 1.
**2nd row:** P to last 6 stitches, k 6. Rep these 2 rows once more, then make a buttonhole.
**5th row:** K 3, wool forward, k 2 tog, k 1, pattern to end.
**6th row:** P to last 6 stitches, k 6. Continue in pattern, keeping the 6 border stitches in garter stitch, and making buttonholes on every 18th

row from previous buttonhole until there are 4 in all. Work 3 rows after last buttonhole, then shape front thus:

**Next row:** K 6, k 2 tog, pattern to end. Continue to decrease inside the front border on every 4th row until the work measures 15cm from beginning, ending with a right-side row.

**Armhole shaping:** Still decreasing at front edge, cast off 5 stitches at beginning of next row, cast off 5 stitches at beginning of next alternate row, then decrease 1 stitch at same edge on next 2 alternate rows. Keeping armhole edge straight, continue to decrease at front edge as before until 26 stitches remain and work measures 25.5cm from beginning, ending with a right-side row.

**Shoulder shaping:** Cast off 10 stitches at beginning of next row and next alternate row. Continue in garter stitch on remaining 6 stitches for 5cm. Cast off.

### LEFT FRONT

Work like the right front, but with all shapings at opposite edges and omitting buttonholes.

### SLEEVES

Cast on 41 stitches and work in pattern, increase 1 stitch at both ends of the 7th row and every 8th row following until there are 65 stitches. Continue without shaping until work measures 23cm from beginning, then shape top by casting off 2 stitches at beginning of next 2 rows, after which decrease 1 stitch at both ends of every row until 41 stitches remain.Cast off.

## JUMPER

### BACK

Cast on 86 stitches and work as given for back of cardigan until work measures 24cm from beginning, ending with a purl row.

**Shoulder shaping:** Cast off 8 stitches at beginning of next 4 rows. Cast off remainder.

### FRONT

Work like the back until work measures 20cm from beginning, ending with a purl row.

**Neck shaping:** Pattern 22, cast off 28, pattern to end. Continue on last set of stitches as follows: Work back to neck, then cast off 2 stitches at beginning of next row, and next alternate row, after which decrease 1 stitch at beginning of next 2 alternate rows. Continue without shaping until work measures 24cm from beginning, ending at armhole edge.

**Shoulder shaping:** Cast off 8 stitches at beginning of next row, and next alternate row. Join wool to neck edge of stitches for other side and work to match first.

### SLEEVES

Cast on 51 stitches and work in pattern, increase 1 stitch at both ends of 3rd row, and every 4th row following until there are 65 stitches. Continue without shaping until work measures 7.5cm from beginning, then shape top as given for sleeves of cardigan.

### NECK

Join right shoulder seam, then with right side of work facing you pick up and knit 98 stitches all round neck edge. Work 3 rows in garter stitch. Cast off.

### MAKING UP

Press work on wrong side. Join shoulder seams of cardigan. Sew in sleeves, then sew up side and sleeve seams. Join neck band at centre back, then sew across back neck. Sew on buttons to correspond with buttonholes. Join left shoulder of jumper for about 2.5cm in from armhole edge. Sew in sleeves, then sew up side and sleeve seams. Work 1 row of DC across back shoulder opening, then work 2 rows across front shoulder opening, but making 2 loops on 2nd row. Sew on buttons to correspond with loops.

Child's bolero with rose trimming in fair isle

# Jennifer

A simple rose turns this plain jacket into a pretty bolero to pop over a dress or blouse.

*Australian Home Journal*, 2 May 1949.

**Materials:** 200g Bendigo Woollen Mills Classic 100% wool 3 ply in Teal; small amounts of red, green and yellow for the fair-isle rose.
1 pair 3.25mm and 3.00mm needles. 3.5mm crochet hook
**Measurements:** Length from shoulder to lower edge, 18cm; sleeve seam, 6cm.
**Tension:** 32 stitches and 40 rows to 10cm.
**Abbreviations:** B=Blue; G=green; Y=yellow; R=red

### BACK

Using the 3.25mm needles and B wool, cast on 80 stitches.
Garter stitch 4 rows.
Change to stocking stitch and work 30 rows.
**Armhole shaping:** Cast off 3 stitches at the beginning of the next 2 rows.
**Next row:** K 2 tog, k to last 2 stitches, k 2 tog
**Next row:** P 2 tog, p to last 2 stitches, k 2 tog
Rep the last 2 rows once more.
**Next row:** K 2 tog, k to last 2 stitches, k 2 tog
**Next row:** P to end.
Repeat the last 2 rows once and the 1st row once. There are now 60 stitches on the needles.
Work 32 rows more in stocking stitch.
Cast off 8 stitches at the beginning of each of the next 2 rows.
Cast off the remainder loosely.

Our knitter suggests using short rows for the shoulders and keeping the stitches on a stitch holder to graft or use a three-needle cast off when joining the fronts and back. To do this, knit to the last 8 stitches, turn; purl to last 8 stitches, turn; knit to last 16 stitches, turn; purl to last 16 stitches; transfer all stitches to a stitch holder. For the front shoulders, work 8 stitches, turn; work to end. Transfer to a stitch holder.

We have added a graph of the fair isle part of the pattern to make it easier to follow, although instructions are written in full in the original pattern. If you prefer, you can embroider the roses onto the bolero after you have knitted it.

## LEFT FRONT

Cast on 40 stitches on 3.25mm needles in B wool and work 4 rows in garter stitch.

**Next row:** K to the end.

**Next row:** K 4, p to the end.

**3rd row:** K 23 B, 2 G, 15 B

**4th row:** K 4 B, p (11 B, 2 G, 1 B, 2 G, 20 B)

**5th row:** K (20 B, 2 G, 1 B, 2 G, 15 B).

**6th row:** K 4 B, p (9 B, 2 G, 1 B, 1 G, 2 B, 1 G, 3 B, 1 G, 16 B)

**7th row:** K (16 B, 1 G, 4 B, 2 G, 1 B, 3 G, 13 B).

**8th row:** K 4 B, p (12 B, 3 G, 3 B, 2 G, 16 B).

**9th row:** K (17 B, 5 G, 18 B).

**10th row:** K 4 B, p (8 B, 2 R, 9 B, 1 G, 16 B).

**11th row:** K (14 B, 2 G, 1 B, 1 G, 7 B, 3 R, 1 B, 2 R, 9 B).

**12th row:** K 4 B, p (5 B, 2 R, 1 B, 3 R, 1 B, 2 R, 3 B, 1 G, 2 B, 1 G, 1 B, 1 G, 13 B).

**13th row:** K (12 B, 1 G, 1 B, 2 G, 3 B, 1 G, 2 B, 2 R, 1 B, 2 R, 1 B, 3 R, 9 B).

**14th row:** K 4 B, p (6 B, 3 R, 2 B, 3 R, 1 B, 1 G, 4 B, 3 G, 1 B, 1 G, 11 B).

**15th row:** K (11 B, 1 G, 1 B, 3 G, 9 B, 2 Y, 2 B, 1 R, 10 B).

**16th row:** K 4 B, p (4 B, 4 R, 1 B, 2 Y, 1 B, 4 R, 4 B, 3 G, 1 B, 1 G, 11 B).

**17th row:** K (11 B, 4 G, 4 B, 4 R, 1 B, 1 R, 3 B, 4 R, 8 B).

**18th row:** K 4 B, p (5 B, 2 R, 2 B, 2 R, 1 B, 1 R, 9 B, 3 G, 11 B).

**19th row:** K (11 B, 1 G, 9 B, 3 R, 1 B, 3 R, 12 B).

**20th row:** K 4 B, p (8 B, 3 R, 1 B, 4 R, 20 B).

**21st row:** K (20 B, 2 R, 4 B, 2 R, 12 B).

This completes the rose. Continue in stocking stitch in all B. Work 9 more rows. (30 rows in stocking stitch in all).

**Shape for the armhole:** Cast off 3 stitches at the beginning of the next row, k to end.

**Next row:** Purl.

Decrease 1 stitch at the armhole edge on the next and each of the following rows for 5 decreases, then decrease twice more on alternate rows. There are now 30 stitches on the needle.

Work 22 rows more in stocking stitch, ending at the neck edge.

**Next row:** Cast off 4 stitches P to the end.

**Next row:** K to last 2 stitches, k 2 tog.

**Next row:** P 2 tog, p to end.

Rep the last 2 rows 3 times (18 stitches).

Work 2 or 3 rows in stocking stitch, ending at the armhole edge.

**Next row:** Cast off 8 stitches, k to the end.

**Next row:** Cast off the remaining 10 stitches in purl.

## RIGHT FRONT

Work as for the Left Front, reversing all shapings and the pattern for the rose, as follows:

**1st row of stocking stitch** K to the end.

**2nd row:** P to last 4 stitches, k 4.

**3rd row:** K (15 B, 2 G, 23 B), etc.

Work 1 additional row in stocking stitch before shaping at the armhole.

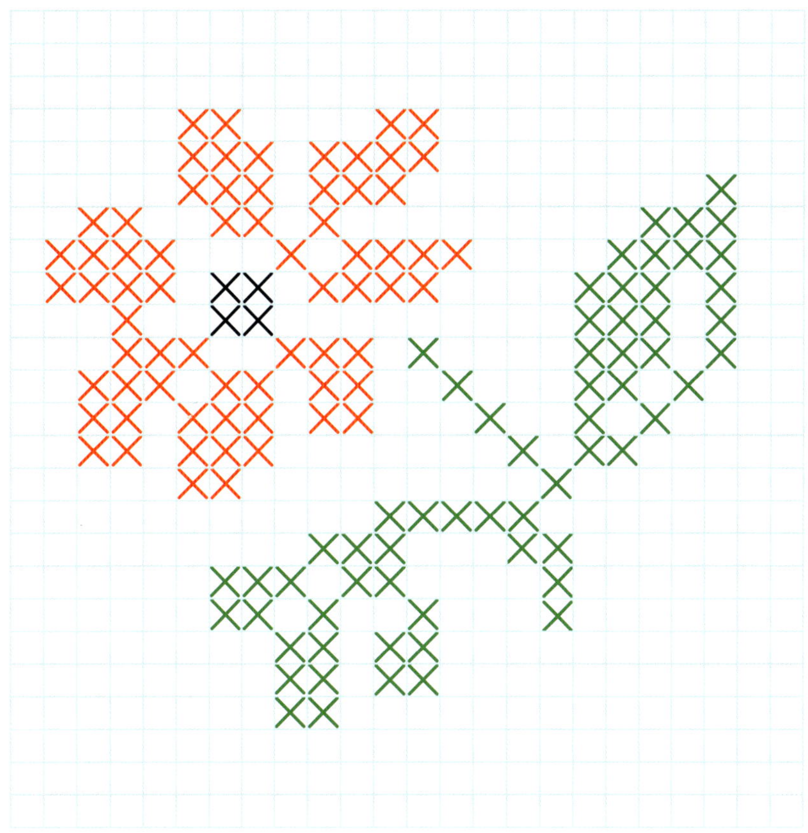

**5th row:** Knit.
Repeat rows 3 to 6 twice more (64 stitches).
**15th row:** as 3rd row.
**16th row:** as 4th row.
Repeat rows 15 and 16 until 28 stitches remain (18 times in total), then decrease at each end of every row until 16 stitches remain. P2 tog across next row (8 stitches).
Cast off.
Work another sleeve to match.

### COLLAR

Cast on 64 stitches on 2.75mm needles in B wool.
**1st row:** Knit.
**2nd row:** K 4, p 56, k 4.
Rep these 2 rows once.
Change to 3.25mm needles and work 10 more rows in stocking stitch, keeping the 4 stitches at each end of the needle in garter stitch as before.
Work 5 more rows in garter stitch.
Cast off loosely.

### SLEEVES

Cast on 68 stitches on 3.25mm needles in B wool.
Starting with a wrong side row, work 4 rows in garter stitch, then 10 rows in reverse stocking stitch commencing with a knit row.
Change to 2.75mm needles and work in stocking stitch, as follows:
**Next row:** P to the end.
**Next row:** K to the end.
Rep the last 2 rows 4 times, p 1 row.
Change to 3.25mm needles and continue to work in stocking stitch. * Increase 1 stitch at the beginning and end of the next row, work 1 row. Repeat from * (72 stitches).
**Shaping of sleeve cap:**
**1st row:** Cast off 1 stitch, knit to end.
**2nd row:** Cast off 1 stitch, purl to end.
**3rd row:** Knit, decreasing 1 stitch at beginning and end of row.
**4th and 6th rows:** Purl.

### TO MAKE UP

Press all stocking stitch parts lightly with a warm iron over a damp cloth. Join the shoulder seams. Join sides and sleeve seams. Sew the sleeves into the armholes, making a pleat each side of the shoulder with the fullness at top of the sleeves. Make 3 small pleats at the back of the neck to give size required. Sew on the collar with the cast-on edge to the neck of the bolero.
Work 2 rows of crochet along the front edges, forming a buttonhole at the top of each front by working 3 DC.
Using double blue wool, crochet a length of chain to thread through the buttonhole loops and tie in a bow. Finish ends with a tiny tassel of all the colours mixed.

Originally knitted in Lincoln Mills 'Daphne' 3 ply wool, we've updated it with Bendigo Woollen Mills Classic 3 ply. Knitted in the size given, it will fit a two- to three-year old.

# Fredrick

Just the thing for those cooler summer days is this neat sleeveless pullover in an intriguing new stitch. With the neck and sleeve bands worked in, it is very quickly knitted.

*Olive Ketels' Exclusive Knitwear for Young Folk*, No.2, 1947.

**Materials:** 200g Bendigo Woollen Mills Classic 3 ply; 1 pair each of 3.25mm and 2.75mm needles.
**Measurements:** Length from top of shoulder, 40.5cm; length underarm, 30.5cm; width around underarm, 56cm.
**Tension:** 28 stitches and 40 rows to 10cm.
**Note:** After casting off any number of stitches, the stitches quoted immediately following do not include the loop remaining on the right-hand needle.

## FRONT

With 2.75mm needles, cast on 90 stitches, and knit 7.5cm in rib of k 2, p 2.
Continue on 3.25mm needles, and knit one row knit and one row purl. Commence pattern:
**1st row:** * P 2, k 2 (knitting into back of stitch), p 2, k 2 (knit into back of stitch), p 1, k 4, k 2 (into back of stitch); * Repeat * to * to end of row.
**2nd row:** * P 5, k 2, p 2, k 2, p 2, k 2, *. Repeat * to * to end of row.
**3rd row:** * P 2, k 2 (into back of stitch), p 2, k 2 (into back of stitch), p 3, k 2, k 2 (into back of stitch) *. Repeat * to* to end of row.
**4th row:** * P 3, k 4, p 2, k 2, p 2, k 2, *. Repeat * to * to end of row.
**5th row:** * P 2, k 2 (into back of stitch), p 2, k 2 (into back of stitch), p 5, k 2 (into back of stitch) *. Repeat * to * to end of row.
**6th row:** Same as fourth row.
**7th row:** Same as third row.
**8th row:** Same as second row.
Repeat these 8 pattern rows seven more times, then knit up till seventh row, so as to commence neck with wrong side facing. Proceed:
**1st row:** Knit 11 moss, p 33, k 2 tog, p 33, moss 11.
**2nd row:** Knit 11 moss, k 32, p 1, k 1, p 1, k 32, moss 11.

**3rd row:** Knit 11 moss, p 31, k 1, p 1, k 1, p 1, k 1, p 31, moss 11.
**4th row:** Knit 11 moss, k 30 (p 1, k 1) three times, p 1, k 30, moss 11.
**5th row:** Knit 11 moss, p 29 (k 1, p 1) four times, k 1, p 29, moss 11.
**6th row:** Knit 11 moss, k 28 (p 1, k 1) five times, p 1, k 28, moss 11.
**7th row:** Cast off 6, moss 4, p 27 (k 1, p 1) six times, k 1, p 27, moss 11.
**8th row:** Cast off 6, moss 4, k 26, (p 1, k 1) seven times, p 1, k 26, moss 5.
**9th row:** Moss 5, p 2 tog, p 24 (p 1 k 1) four times. (Divide stitches for neck).
**10th row:** Turn work, cast off 1, (k 1, p 1) three times, k 25, moss 5.
**11th row:** Moss 5, p 2 tog, p 23, moss 7.
**12th row:** Moss 7, k 2 tog, k 22, moss 5.
**13th row:** Moss 5, p 23, moss 7.
**14th row:** Moss 7, k 23, moss 5.
**15th row:** Moss 5, p 2 tog, p 21, moss 7.
**16th row:** Moss 7, k 22, moss 5.
**17th row:** Moss 5, p 22, moss 7.
**18th row:** Moss 7, k 2 tog, k 20, moss 5.
**19th row:** Moss 5, p 21, moss 7.
**20th row:** Moss 7, k 21, moss 5.
Repeat 19th and 20th rows, and then 19th.
**24th row:** Moss 7, k 2 tog, k 19, moss 5.
**25th row:** Moss 5, p 20, moss 7.
**26th row:** Moss 7, k 20, moss 5.
Repeat 25th and 26th rows and then 25th.
**30th row:** Moss 7, k 2 tog, k 18, moss 5.
**31st row:** Moss 5, p 19, moss 7.
**32nd row:** Moss, 7, k 19, moss 5.
**33rd row:** Moss 5, p 19, moss 7.
**34th row:** Moss 7, k 2 tog, k 17, moss 5.
**35th row:** Moss 5, p 18, moss 7.
**36th row:** Moss 7, k 18, moss 5.
**37th row:** Moss 5, p 18, moss 7.
**38th row:** Moss 7, k 2 tog, k 16, moss 5.

**39th row:** Moss 5, p 17, moss 7.
**40th row:** Moss 7, k 17, moss 5.
**41st row:** Moss 5, p 17, moss 7.
**42nd row:** Moss 7, k 2 tog, k 15, moss 5.
**43rd row:** Moss 5, p 16, moss 7.
**44th row:** Moss 7, k 16, moss 5.
**45th row:** Moss 5, p 16, moss 7.
**46th row:** Moss 7, k 2 tog, k 14, moss 5.
**47th row:** Moss 5, p 15, moss 7.
**48th row:** Moss 7, k 15, moss 5.
**49th row:** Moss 5, p 15, moss 7.
**50th row:** Moss 7, k 2 tog, k 13, moss 5.
**51st row:** Moss 5, p 14, moss 7.
**52nd row:** Moss 7, k 14, moss 5.
**53rd row:** Moss 5, p 14, moss 7.
**54th row:** Moss 7, k 2 tog, k 12, moss 5.
**55th row:** Cast off 10, p 8, moss 5.
**56th row:** Moss 7, k 2 tog, k 6.
**57th row:** Cast off 7, moss to end of row.
Continue on these 7 stitches, knitting 5cm in moss stitch.
Cast off *(or put the stitches on a stitch holder to graft together later)*.
Take the other 38 stitches and proceed:
**1st row:** Moss 7, p 26, moss 5.
**2nd row:** Moss 5, k 2 tog, k 24, moss 7.
**3rd row:** Moss 7, p 2 tog, p 23, moss 5.
**4th row:** Moss 5, k 24, moss 7.
**5th row:** Moss 7, p 24, moss 5.
**6th row:** Moss 5, k 2 tog, k 22, moss 7.
**7th row:** Moss 7, p 2 tog, p 21, moss 5.
**8th row:** Moss 5, k 22, moss 7.

**9th row:** Moss 7, p 22, moss 5.
**10th row:** Moss 5, k 20, k 2 tog, moss 7.
**11th row:** Moss 7, p 21, moss 5.
**12th row:** Moss 5, k 21, moss 7.
**13th row:** Repeat 11th and 12th rows, then 11th.
**17th row:** Moss 5, k 19, k 2 tog, moss 7.
**18th row:** Moss 7, p 20, moss 5.
**19th row:** Moss 5, k 20, moss 7.
**20th row:** Repeat 18th and 19th rows, then 18th.
**23rd row:** Moss 5, k 18, k 2 tog, moss 7.
**24th row:** Moss 7, p 19, moss 5.
**25th row:** Moss 5, k 19, moss 7.
**26th row:** Moss 7, p 19, moss 5.
**27th row:** Moss 5, k 17, k 2 tog, moss 7.
**28th row:** Moss 7, p 18, moss 5.
**29th row:** Moss 5, k 18, moss 7.
**30th row:** Moss 7, p 18, moss 5.
**31st row:** Moss 5, k 16, k 2 tog, moss 7.
**32nd row:** Moss 7, p 17, moss 5.
**33rd row:** Moss 5, k 17, moss 7.
**34th row:** Moss 7, p 17, moss 5.
**35th row:** Moss 5, k 15, k 2 tog, moss 7.
**36th row:** Moss 7, p 16, moss 5.
**37th row:** Moss 5, k 16, moss 7.
**38th row:** Moss 7, p 16, moss 5.
**39th row:** Moss 5, k 14, k 2 tog, moss 7.
**40th row:** Moss 7, p 15, moss 5.
**41st row:** Moss 5, k 15, moss 7.
**42nd row:** Moss 7, p 15, moss 5.
**43rd row:** Moss 5, k 13, k 2 tog, moss 7.
**44th row:** Moss 7, p 14, moss 5.
**45th row:** Moss 5, k 14, moss 7.
**46th row:** Moss 7, p 14, moss 5.
**47th row:** Moss 5, k 12, k 2 tog, moss 7.
**48th row:** Moss 7, p 13, moss 5.
**49th row:** Cast off 10, k 7, moss 7.
**50th row:** Moss 7, p 2 tog, p 6.
**51st row:** Cast off 7, moss to end.
Continue on remaining 7 stitches and knit 5cm moss stitch.
Cast off *(or place the stitches on a stitch holder to graft together later).*

## BACK

Knit as directed for front until pattern section is completed, then proceed:
**1st row:** Moss 11, p 68, moss 11.
**2nd row:** Moss 11, k 68, moss 11.
Repeat these two rows twice.
**7th row:** Cast off 6, moss 4, p 68, moss 11.
**8th row:** Cast off 6, moss 4, k 68, moss 5.
**9th row:** Moss 5, p 68, moss 5.
**10th row:** Moss 5, k 68, moss 5.
Repeat 9th and 10th rows until armholes measure 14cm.
**Next row:** Moss 5, k 22, cast off 24, k 21, moss 5.
**Next row:** Cast off 10, p 14, p 2 tog.
**Next row:** Cast off 5, k to end of row.
Cast off.
Take other side and proceed: p 2 tog, p 20, moss 5.
**Next row:** Cast off 10, k to last 2 stitches, k 2 tog.
**Next row:** Cast off 5, purl to end of row.
Cast off.

## TO MAKE UP GARMENT

Finish off all ends securely with darning needle. Sew up shoulder seams and join neckband. Sew band neatly across back of neck and sew up side seams.
Press seams out flat, then press yoke lightly with damp cloth.

# Literary knitters

Knitting in literature often represents domesticity, creativity and generosity, but is occasionally used as a camouflage for hidden motives.

A woman knits in a wine shop in this illustration from an 1859 edition of *A Tale of Two Cities* by Charles Dickens

In Jane Austen's novel, *Persuasion*, Mrs Smith displays her creativity and kindheartedness:

> *As soon as I could use my hands, she taught me to knit, which has been a great amusement; and she put me in the way of making these little thread-cases, pincushions and card-racks, which you always find me so busy about, and which supply me with the means of doing a little good to one or two very poor families in this neighbourhood.*

Mrs Weasley in J.K. Rowling's Harry Potter series knits sweaters every Christmas for all of her children and Harry, incorporating designs that represent each individual.

Madame Defarge in Charles Dicken's novel *A Tale of Two Cities*, is one of les Tricoteuses (see page 106). She knits as she watches the public beheadings in Paris, while covertly encoding the names of the guillotined enemies of the Revolution into her knitting.

Agatha Christie's Miss Marple passes for a little old lady happily occupied with her knitting, while quietly observing and analysing everything going on about her. In *The Blood-Stained Pavement*, Miss Marple notes that, 'Sitting here with one's knitting, one just sees the facts'.

In *Little Women* by Louisa May Alcott, we catch glimpses of the March sisters knitting socks for soldiers in the American Civil War. In these excerpts, knitting seems to help them deal with their feelings:

> *Beth said nothing, but wiped away her tears with the blue army sock and began to knit with all her might, losing no time in doing the duty that lay nearest her ... But Jo had her own eyes to take care of, and feeling that they could not be trusted, she prudently kept them on the little sock she was knitting, like a model maiden aunt. A stealthy glance now and then refreshed her like sips of fresh water after a dusty walk.*

# Josephine

This cardigan is worked sideways, allowing garter stitch to create vertical stripes. The sleeves are also knitted sideways separately and set in.

*What Children Wear in Knitting and Crochet* by Ella Allen, Melbourne: Specialty Press, 1930–1931.

**Materials:** 150g Bellevue Park Wool 4 ply 100% superfine merino wool. 1 pair each of 4.00mm and 3.25mm needles.

## BODY

Begin at left side and cast on 60 stitches.
**1st row:** Knit 1 row.
**2nd row:** K 1, increase (by knitting into front then into back of next stitch); knit to end.
**3rd row:** Knit.
Knit 7 more rows, increasing at beginning of even rows as before to shape neck.
**Pattern stripes:**
**1st row:** K 6, * p 2, k 2 * alternately to end of row.
**2nd row:** K 2 * p 2, k 2 * to last 6 stitches, k 6.
Repeat these 2 rows 2 more times (6 rows of pattern).
**Garter stitch stripes:**
**1st row:** Knit.
**2nd row:** Knit. Repeat these 2 rows 4 more times (10 rows of garter stitch).
Repeat these stripes the whole way, continuing to increase at the top edge until you have 78 stitches on needle.
You are now about to knit the 3rd rib of a garter stitch stripe and commence the shoulder. Continue in the stripes as before without increasing until you are about to knit 3rd rib of 5th garter stitch stripe (where shoulder ends).
**Armhole shaping:** Cast off 22 stitches and knit to end of row. Knit to underarm, then, in knitting 4th and 5th ribs, decrease by knitting 2nd and 3rd stitches together.
Knit pattern stripe as usual, then increase at underarm on first 2 ribs of garter stitch stripe. Knit to underarm and cast on 22 stitches. You have now 78 stitches again on needle.
Knit as for 1st shoulder. When you have completed 3rd rib of 8th garter stitch stripe

Four-ply fingering wool was the original recommendation for this cardigan; our updated version is in a beautifully soft superfine merino wool, still in 4 ply.

from beginning, reduce at neck in 5th rib. Finish stripe, then pattern stripe, in each of the next two garter stitch stripes work as follows:

**In 3rd and 5th rows** of stripe knit 68, turn, slip 1, knit to end.

**Other rows:** Knit right to the end of needle. This will make neck a little narrower as you will have 3 ribs instead of 5 at neck edge.

In 2nd rib of 11th garter stitch stripe, increase at neck then work 3rd shoulder, armhole, and 4th shoulder, afterwards decreasing 1 stitch each time at neck edge until you are reduced to 60 stitches as at beginning. Cast off.

## SLEEVE

Cast on 40 stitches and knit in stripes the same as before, but have 3 ribs instead of 5 at beginning and end of sleeve, and without 6 knit stitches at wrist edge, increasing at shoulder edge until you have 52 stitches, then without increase until you are about to knit 6th row of pattern stripe, then decrease at the shoulder edge until reduced to 40 stitches. Cast off. Take a pair of 3.25mm needles and pick up stitches at wrist edge. Knit in rib of k 2, p 2, for about 5cm.

## MAKE UP

Graft or sew shoulder seams together. Sew underarm seam of sleeves and sew sleeves in to armholes.

## COLLAR

Pick up and knit all stitches around neck from beginning of one slope to end of other and knit in plain, knitting 20 rows of garter stitch (10 ribs) and cast off. Sew buttons on front.

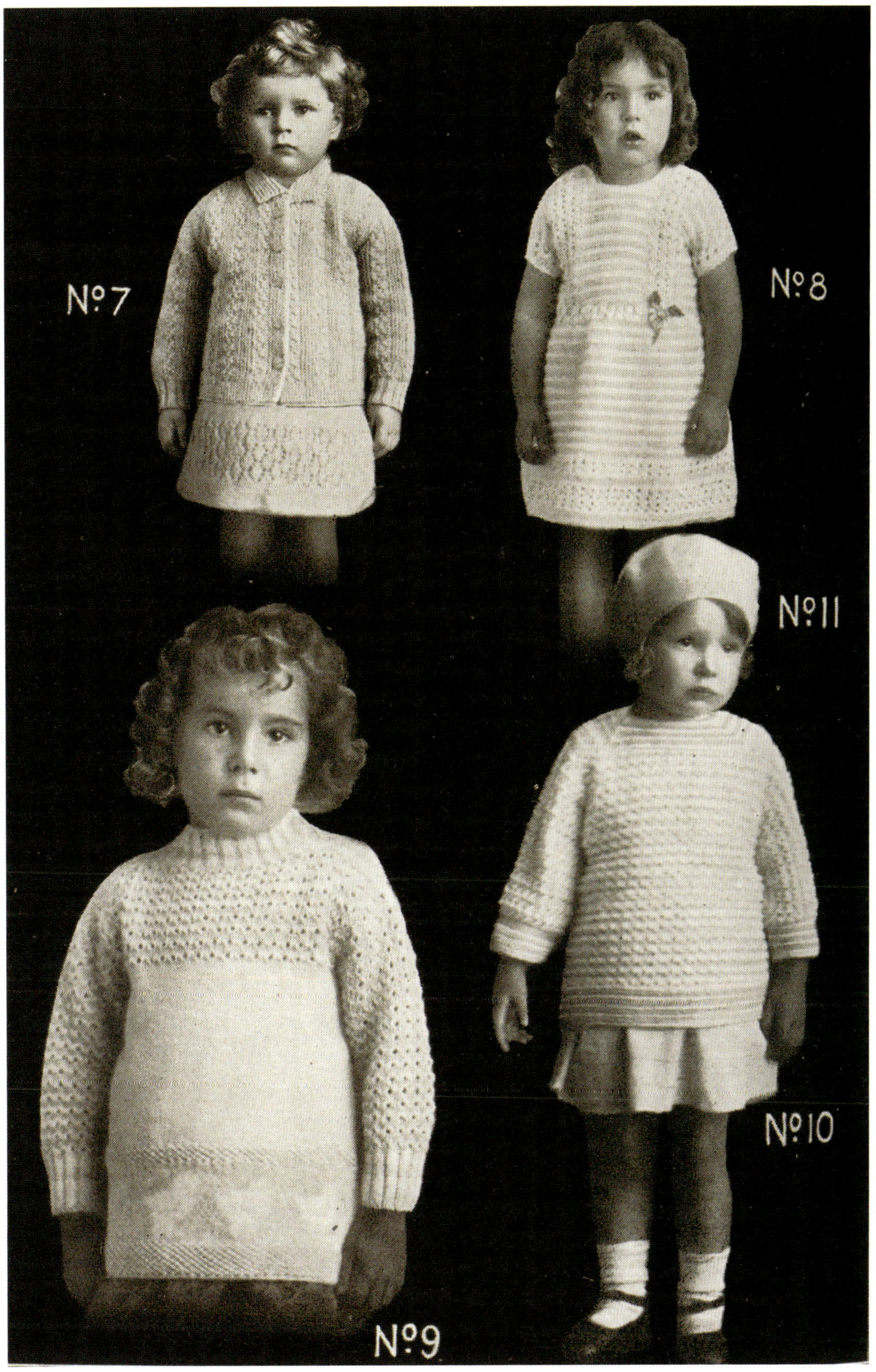
No.7
No.8
No.11
No.10
No.9

The original pattern called for 2 ply yarn, but we found that 4 ply gave the correct tension for this garment. The stripes of the crayons are knitted horizontally and the spaces between them are embroidered with herringbone stitch.

# David

Crayons are a favourite with preschoolers, and this motif is easy to knit into a cute cardigan for a two- to four-year old.

*Australian Home Journal*, 1 August 1952.

**Materials:** 200g Patons Dreamtime Merino 4 ply 100% Australian fine merino wool in grey; 50g in blue; small amounts of three contrasting colours (C1, C2, C3) for the crayon stripes. 1 pair of 3.25mm knitting needles. 3.5mm crochet hook. 6 buttons.
**Measurements:** Length, 33cm; width at underarm, 56cm; sleeve seam, 28cm.
**Tension:** 36 stitches and 48 rows to 10cm.
**Abbreviations:** G, grey; B, blue.

## CRAYON PATTERN

Work 4 rows in stocking stitch with blue (B) wool, 4 rows grey (G), 4 rows C1, 4 rows grey, 4 rows C2, 4 rows grey, 4 rows C3, 4 rows grey, then proceed in grey (G) and blue (B):
**Row 33:** * K 2 G, 7 B; repeat from * to last 2 stitches, 2 G.
**Row 34:** * P 2 G, 7 B; repeat from * to last 2 stitches, 2 G.
**Row 35:** * K 3 G, 5 B, 1 G; repeat from * to last 2 stitches, 2 G.
**Row 36:** P 2 G *, 1 G, 5 B, 3 G; repeat from * to end of row.
**Row 37:** *K 4 G, 3 B, 2 G; repeat from * to last 2 stitches, 2 G.
**Row 38:** P 2 G, *2 G, 3 B, 4 G; repeat from * to end of row.
**Row 39:** * K 5 G, 1 B, 3 G; repeat from * to last 2 stitches, 2 G.
**Row 40:** P 2 G, * 3 G, 1 B, 5 G; repeat from * to end of row.
This completes the pattern.

## BACK

Cast on 76 stitches in grey and work 6.5cm in k 1, p 1 ribbing.
**Next row:** K and increase 16 stitches evenly across row (92 stitches).
**Next row:** Purl 1 row.

Continue in stocking stitch. Work 2 rows in G. Work crayon pattern once and then continue in G only. When work measures 20cm, shape armholes. Cast off 3 stitches at each end of next row, then work 1 purl row. Cast off 2 stitches at each end of next and alternate rows 3 times (74 stitches). Purl 1 row between each cast-off row. Continue straight until back measures 33cm. Cast off.

## RIGHT FRONT

Cast on 49 stitches in G. Work a border of 9 stitches in garter stitch and work k 1, p 1 ribbing on the other 40 stitches. When border is 2.5cm long, make first buttonhole. Starting on border stitches k 3, k 2 tog, yrn, k 4, finish row.
When border measures 6.5cm, work next row, starting at border edge as follows: k 2, k 2 tog, yrn, k 4 (second buttonhole), * k 2, increase in next stitch; repeat from * 10 times more, knit to end of row (60 stitches).

**Next row:** P 51, k 9.
**Next row:** K 9 and put these border stitches on a safety pin or stitch holder, knit to end of row.
Purl 1 row.
Work Pattern once, then continue in grey only.
When front measures 20cm, start armhole and neckline shaping in next wrong-side row: cast off 3, p to 2 stitches from end of row, p 2 tog.
Further cast off at armhole edge 3, 2, 1 stitches more and repeat decrease for neckline 12 more times every 4th row.
Continue straight on 30 stitches until front measures 33cm. Cast off.
Pick up border stitches from safety pin. Continue in garter stitch, making four more buttonholes with 3cm between each. When border measures 37cm, cast off.

## LEFT FRONT

Work in reverse to correspond to right front, omitting buttonholes.

**SLEEVES**

Cast on 50 stitches and work 5cm in k 1, p 1 ribbing.

**Next row:** K and increase 24 stitches evenly across row (74 stitches).

**Next row:** Purl 1 row.

Now work pattern once, but work 2 rows of each colour instead of 4. Continue in grey only and increase 1 stitch at both ends of row every 1.25cm until there are 88 stitches. Continue straight until sleeve measures 28cm.

**Shape top:** Cast off at both sides 2 stitches 7 times, 1 stitch 6 times, 2 stitches 7 times. Cast off remaining 16 stitches.

**FINISHING**

Press parts lightly under damp cloth, avoiding ribbing. Join seams and sew in sleeves. Sew borders along each front and along back neck, weaving ends of border together at centre back neck. Work embroidery: herringbone stitch in blue over two stitches between each triangle down to the border (as illustrated). Sew on buttons.

# Douglas

Twin sets are ideal for two-year olds, and youngsters adore the quaint rabbit motifs.

*Olive Ketels' Exclusive Knitwear for Young Folk*, No.2, 1947.

**Materials:** 250g Bendigo Woollen Mills Luxury 100% wool, 4 ply. 1 pair each of 3.25mm, 2.75mm and 2.00mm needles. 6 buttons.
**Measurements:** Full length, 33cm; underarm, 19cm; sleeves, 20cm (with 2.5cm cuff); width around underarm, 51cm. A larger size may be obtained by using 3.75mm needles.
**Tension**: 28 stitches to 10cm.

## JUMPER

### FRONT

With light grey wool and 2.75mm needles, cast on 68 stitches and knit 5cm in rib as follows:
**1st row:** *K 1 (knitting into back of stitch), p 1; * repeat * to * to end of row.
**2nd row:** *K 1, p 1; * repeat * to * to end of row.
Change to 3.25mm needles and knit 15cm stocking stitch Cast off 4 at beginning of next two rows for armholes, then k 2 tog at beginning of following two rows. Knit 6 rows stocking stitch.

Proceed to work motif as follows:
f = light grey
b = dark grey
**1st row:** Knit 23 f, 6 b, 29 f.
**2nd row:** Purl 20 f, 7 b, 2 f, 8 b, 21 f.
**3rd row:** Knit 20 f, 6 b, 5 f, 5 b, 22 f.
**4th row:** Purl 22 f, 17 b, 19 f.
**5th row:** Knit 18 f, 19 b, 21 f.
**6th row:** Purl 19 f, 21 b, 18 f.
**7th row:** Knit 18 f, 22 b, 18 f.
**8th row:** Purl 18 f, 22 b, 18 f.
**9th row:** Knit 19 f, 21 b, 18 f.
**10th row:** Purl 19 f, 2 b, 1 f, 16 b, 20 f.
**11th row:** Knit 21 f, 9 b, 1 f, 8 b, 19 f.
**12th row:** Purl 20 f, 6 b, 3 f, 7 b, 22 f.
**13th row:** Knit 31 f, 4 b, 23 f.
**14th row:** Purl 24 f, 4 b, 30 f.
**15th row:** Knit 29 f, 2 b, 1 f, 2 b, 24 f.
**16th row:** Purl 24 f, p 2 b tog, p 1 f, p 2 b tog, p 20 f (56 sts).

Six skeins of fawn Paton's 'AZALEA' crochet wool plus a small quantity of light brown were recommended for this cute ensemble. We updated with 4 ply 100% wool. The rabbit motifs are intarsia (knitted in), but you could embroider them on later if you prefer.

**17th row:** Knit
**18th row:** Purl
Continue in stocking stitch until armhole measures 10cm along straight edge, then proceed as follows:
**1st row:** Knit 12, knit 32 in moss stitch (commencing p 1, k 1), knit 12.
**2nd row:** Purl 12, knit 32 in moss stitch, p 12.
Repeat these two rows three times, then 1st row.
**10th row:** P 12 (k 1, p 1) three times, k 1, cast off 18, (k 1, p 1) three times, p 12.
Continuing on these 19 stitches:
**11th row:** K 12 (p 1, k 1) three times, p 1.
**12th row:** (P 1, k 1) three times, p 13.
Repeat 11th and 12th rows.
**15th row:** K 12, p 1, k 1, cast off 3, p 1.
**16th row:** P 1, k 1, cast on 3, k 1, p 13.
**17th row:** K 12 (p 1, k 1) three times, p 1.
Cast off. Knit other shoulder to correspond.

### BACK

Knit as given for front until decreases for armholes are completed, then continue in stocking stitch until armhole measures 10cm along straight edge, and proceed:
**1st row:** K 11, k 2 tog, k 32 in moss stitch, (commencing p 1, k 1), k 2 tog, k 12.
**2nd row:** P 12, moss 32, p 12.
Repeat these 2 rows 4 times.
**11th row:** Same as 1st row.
**12th row:** P 12 (k 1, p 1) three times, k 1, cast off 18, (k 1, p 1) three times, p 12.
Continuing on these 19 stitches:
**13th row:** K 12 (p 1, k 1) three times, p 1.
**14th row:** (P 1, k 1) three times, p 13.
Repeat 13th and 14th rows twice. Cast off.
Knit other shoulder to correspond.

### SLEEVES

With 2.00mm needles cast on 37 stitches and knit 2.5cm in moss stitch, then 2.5cm in rib of k 1, p 1, knitting 2 tog at the beginning of first row of rib.
**Next row:** Knit twice into every second stitch to end of row (54 stitches).
**Next row:** Purl.
Change to 3.25mm needles and knit in stocking stitch until work measures 23cm, then proceed:
Cast off 3 stitches at beginning of next two rows, and continue in stocking stitch, knitting 2 tog at beginning and end of every next and alternate row 9 times, then in every row until 22 stitches remain. Cast off.
Knit other sleeve to match.

### MAKE UP

With darning needle, finish off all ends securely. Sew up side seams, then shoulder seams, leaving a placket of 3cm each side of neck. When sewing up sleeve seams, sew the moss-stitch cuff with right side of work out. Insert sleeves, work around buttonholes and sew buttons on shoulders. Press seams flat and press motif with damp cloth.

## CARDIGAN

### BACK

Using 3.25mm needles, cast on 73 stitches and knit 8 rows in moss stitch.
Change to 3.75mm needles and knit in stocking stitch until work measures 20cm, then shape armholes by casting off 3 stitches at beginning of next two rows.
Knit 6 rows in stocking stitch, then k 2 tog at beginning of next two rows.
Continue in stocking stitch until armhole measures 14cm along straight edge.
Shape shoulders by casting off 6 stitches at beginning of next six rows.
Cast off.

### RIGHT FRONT

Using 3.25mm needles, cast on 39 stitches and knit 8 rows in moss stitch. Change to 3.75mm needles.
**9th row:** Moss 5, knit 34.
**10th row:** Purl 34, moss 5.
Repeat 9th and 10th rows until work measures 19cm, finishing with a purl row, then proceed:
**1st row:** Moss 5, k 2 tog, k 32.
**2nd row:** Purl 33, moss 5.
**3rd row:** Moss 5, k 33.

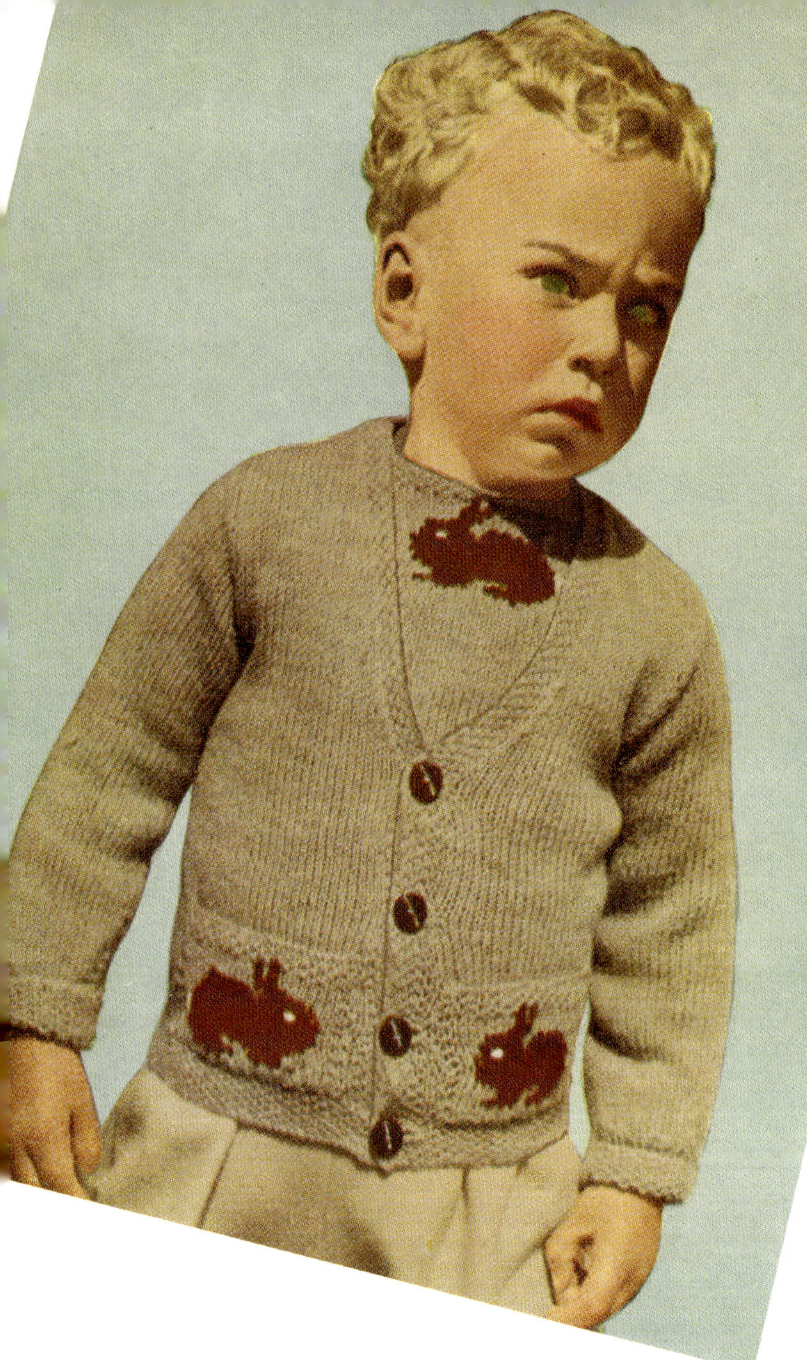


**4th row:** Purl 33, moss 5.
**5th row:** Moss 5, k 2 tog, k 31.
**6th row:** Purl 32, moss 5.
**7th row:** Moss 5, k 32.
**8th row:** Cast off 5, p 26, moss 5.
**9th row:** Moss 5, k 2 tog, k 25.
Knit 2 tog at beginning of next 3 purl rows, and continue decreasing inside the border every 4th row until 23 stitches remain. When armhole measures 14cm, shape shoulder by casting off 6 stitches at beginning of next 3 purl rows. Knit 3.5cm moss stitch on remaining 5 stitches. Cast off.

## LEFT FRONT

Using 3.25mm needles, Cast on 39 stitches and knit 4 rows in moss stitch.
**5th row:** Moss 34, cast off 3, k 1.
**6th row:** Moss 2, cast on 3, moss 34.
Knit 2 rows moss stitch Change to 3.75mm needles.
**9th row:** K 34, moss 5.
**10th row:** Moss 5, p 34.
Making a buttonhole every 5cm, repeat 9th and 10th rows until work measures 19cm, then proceed:
**1st row:** K 32, k 2 tog, moss 5.
**2nd row:** Moss 5, p 33.
**3rd row:** K 33, moss 5.
**4th row:** Moss 5, p 33.
**5th row:** K 31, k 2 tog, moss 5.
**6th row:** Moss 5, p 32.

**7th row:** Cast off 5, k 26, moss 5.
**8th row:** Moss 5, p 27.
**9th row:** Knit 25, k 2 tog, moss 5.
Knit 2 tog at beginning of next 3 knit rows, and continue decreasing inside the border every 4th row until 23 stitches remain. When armhole measures 14cm along the straight side, shape shoulder by casting off 6 stitches at beginning of next 3 knit rows. Knit 3.5cm moss stitch on remaining 5 stitches. Cast off.

## SLEEVES

Knit as directed for jumper.

## POCKETS

**RIGHT:** With light grey wool and 3.25mm needles, cast on 28 stitches and knit 2 rows in garter stitch, then proceed:
**1st row:** Knit 14 f, 6 b, 8 f.
**2nd row:** K 2 f, p 4 f, 8 b, 2 f, 7 b, 3 f, k 2 f.
**3rd row:** K 7 f, 5 b, 5 f, 6 b, 5 f.
**4th row:** K 2 f, p 2 f, 17 b, 5 f, k 2 f.
**5th row:** K 6 f, 19 b, 3 f.
**6th row:** K 2 f, p 2 f, 20 b, 2 f, k 2 f.
**7th row:** K 3 f, 22 b, 3 f.
**8th row:** K 2 f, p 1 f, 22 b, 1 f, k 2 f.
**9th row:** K 3 f, 21 b, 4 f.
**10th row:** K 2 f, p 3 f, 16 b, 1 f, 2 b, 2 f, k 2 f.
**11th row:** K 4 f, 8 b, 1 f, 9 b, 6 f.
**12th row:** K 2 f, p 15 f, 6 b, 3 f, k 2 f.
**13th row:** K 8 f, 4 b, 16 f.
**14th row:** K 2 f, p 13 f, 4 b, / t, k 2 f.
**15th row:** K 9 f, 2 b, 1 f, 2 b, 14 f.
**16th row:** K 2 f, p 12 f, p 2 tog, 1 f, p 2 tog, p 7 f, k 2 f.
**17th row:** K 9 f, 1 b, 1 f, 1 b, 14 f.
**18th row:** K tog, purl to end.
Knit 3 rows moss stitch.
Cast off.
**LEFT:** Cast on 28 stitches and knit two rows garter stitch, then proceed:
**1st row:** Knit 8 f, 6 b, 14 f.
**2nd row:** K 2 f, p 3 f, 7 b, 2 f, 8 b, 4 f, k 2 f.
**3rd row:** K 5 f, 6 b, 5 f, 5 b, 7 f.
**4th row:** K 2 f, p 5 f, 17 b, 2 f, k 2 f.
**5th row:** K 3 f, 19 b, 6 f.
**6th row:** K 2 f, p 2 f, 21 b, 1 f, k 2 f.
**7th row:** K 3 f, 22 b, 3 f.
**8th row:** K 2 f, p 1 f, 22 b, 1 f, k 2 f.
**9th row:** K 4 f, 21 b, 3 f.
**10th row:** K 2 f, p 2 f, 2 b, 1 f, 16 b, 3 f, k 2 f.
**11th row:** K 6 f, 9 b, 1 f, 8 b, 4 f.
**12th row:** K 2 f, p 3 f, 6 b, 15 f, k 2 f.
**13th row:** K 16 f, 4 b, 8 f.
**14th row:** K 2 f, p 7 f, 4 b, 13 f, k 2 f.
**15th row:** K 14 f, 2 b, 1 f, 2 b, 9 f.
**16th row:** K 2 f, p 7 f, p 2 b tog, p 1 f, p 2 b tog, p 12 f, k 2 f.
**17th row:** K 14 f, 1 b, 1 f, 1 b, 9 f.
**18th row:** K 2 tog, purl to end.
Knit three rows moss stitch.
Cast off.

## MAKE UP

Finish off all ends securely with darning needle, and press pieces out flat. Sew up shoulder seams, side seams and sleeve seams, being careful to stitch the cuff with right side of work out. Insert sleeves, and join moss stitch band at back. Stitch neatly across back of neck.
Sew on pockets, turning 5mm under all round.
Work around buttonholes, sew on buttons and work eyes in rabbits.
Press seams flat.

# A brief history of knitting

Knitting is different from the more ancient art of weaving, which uses at least two separate yarns, each woven through the entire length of the fabric at right angles to the other. Knitted fabrics have courses or rows. These rows are parallel, in one plane, and attached to each other through loops in the yarn.

The term 'knitting' first entered the English language in the late sixteenth century, denoting the textile handcraft we know as knitting, using two or more needles. The very old craft of 'nalbinding', with archeological examples found in Africa and Scandinavia, uses only one needle and is generally not considered true knitting; nevertheless, some historians consider nalbinding to be the forerunner of knitting, which superseded it between the fifth and twelfth centuries.

Because knitting stitches are worked from right to left in a similar fashion to Arabic script, knitting is thought to have started in the Middle East. Knitting in medieval Europe is connected to the presence of Islamic religion and culture in Spain. Knitted cushions, possibly half-silk and bearing Arabic-Islamic words, have been found in a tomb in northern Spain dated to the thirteenth century. Knitted cotton stockings from Egypt, dated to between the thirteenth and sixteenth century, carry Arabic script including the word 'Allah' or God.

Knitting spread to Europe possibly through the Crusades (1096–1291) and Mediterranean trade routes.

### Materials

Early materials used for knitting include yarns of cotton, silk and wool. Early knitting needles were generally made of metal. European knitters used steel while eastern Mediterranean countries used brass. In Britain, steel was used up until the eighteenth century, but by the mid-nineteenth century, materials such as ivory and whalebone were introduced as alternatives.

Today's handknitters can select from materials such as plastic, bamboo, tortoiseshell and vulcanite or hardened rubber, which make it possible to choose a needle in a colour to contrast with the yarn. Aluminium is used for making lightweight needles.

### Stitches and styles

The first form of knitting was tubular stockinette or stocking stitch, used for making stockings in the round. Knit only in the plain knit stitch, the same side of the fabric faces the knitter throughout the task, and the courses or rows end up becoming a spiral. Medieval samples of knitting are almost always done in the round on double-pointed needles.

The purl stitch was developed later, possibly as a means to turn the heel on a stocking. Plain and purl are, in fact, not different stitches but represent the two sides of the basic interlooping stitch. Mid-sixteenth-century Europeans used mixed plain and purl in stockings and to create patterns resembling woven damask, a luxury fabric with dramatic designs. Fragments of knitting from ancient times show signs of ribbing and cabling.

TOP These Egyptian socks (dated to between 300 and 499 AD) were created using nalbinding, which has the same fabric structure as knitting, but is created using just one needle; RIGHT The Madonna is creating a shirt using four double-pointed needles in this painting dated to about 1405.

'It's designed to be made in white or a pastel tone. If white isn't your first choice, we suggest primrose or pale blue. Make jersey and knickers in same colour for best effect,' said the original instructions, for an outfit knitted in Nursery Viyella wool.

To bring this outfit up to date, we've chosen colours that a modern parent will love, in a yarn from Jawoll. Our knitter found that using 3.00mm and 2.75mm needles gave the correct tension.

# Ian

This jumper suit will fit a child of about one year, boy or girl. It's such an unusually charming design, you'll find it a joy to knit.

*The Australian Women's Weekly*, 23 March 1940.

**Materials:** 150g Lang Yarns Jawoll Superwash 75% wool, 25% nylon 4 ply yarn in mustard (0339) and 100g Jawoll Superwash in royal blue (0235); 1 pair of 3.25mm and 3.00mm knitting needles; 46cm narrow dress elastic; 6 small buttons.

**Measurements:** To fit a child 1-2 years old. Jersey: Length, 33cm; width all round 56cm. Length of sleeve and shoulder from neck, including cuff, 39cm. Length of sleeve seam, including cuff, 32cm. Knickers: Length down centre front, 29cm. Length down centre back, 32cm. Width across widest part, 30cm.

**Tension:** 28 stitches and 36 rows to 10cm.

## JERSEY

### BACK

Using 3.00mm needles, begin at the lower edge by casting on 80 stitches. Work 25 rows in k 1, p 1 rib, working into the backs of the stitches on the first row. Change to 3.25mm needles and the following pattern:

**1st row:** K 1, *p 3, k 2, rep from * all across, ending k 1.

**2nd row:** P, 1, * K 3, p 2, rep from * all across, ending p 1.

**3rd row:** As 1st row.

**4th row:** P 1, * pick up the loop lying between the stitch just worked and the next one—knitwise—then k 3, pass the picked-up loop over the 3 stitches just knitted, p 2, rep from * all across, ending with a p 1.

Repeat these 4 rows for the pattern and proceed without shaping till the work measures 24cm from beginning (including ribbing).

Shape the armholes by decreasing the edge stitches at both ends on each of the next 9 rows (62 stitches). Work without decrease on these stitches for 5cm.

**Next row:** Work 16 stitches, cast off 30 stitches, work 16 stitches. Work for 3.5cm without decrease on the last 16 stitches, finishing at end of 4th row of pattern.
Change to garter stitch and work for 1.25cm. Cast off.
Join wool to inside edge of opposite side and work to correspond.

### FRONT

Work exactly as for back till work measures 2.5cm past armhole shaping.
**Next row:** Work 16 stitches, cast off 30 stitches, work 16 stitches. Work on the last 16 stitches till armhole edge is same depth as back, not including the garter-stitch band. Cast off.
Join the wool to inside edge of opposite side and work to correspond.

### SLEEVES (BOTH ALIKE)

Using 3.00mm needles, cast on 46 stitches work 25 rows in (k 1, p, 1) rib, working into the backs of the stitches on the 1st row, and decreasing 1 stitch at end of last row of ribbing.
Change to 3.25mm needles and main pattern and work 9 rows straight.
On next and every following 7th row increase in the edge stitch at both ends of needle till there are 65 stitches, on the needle. Work 4 rows straight.
Shape the top by decrease the edge stitches at both ends of needle till 35 stitches remain. Cast off.

### NECK RIBBING

Using 3.00mm needles and holding the right side of the work towards you pick up and knit through every stitch and the edge of every row round the back of the neck, including the garter-stitch bands. On the original there were 66 stitches in all.
Work 1 row in k 1, p 1 rib. Continue in the ribbing and on next row work 3 stitches together on both inner corners. Repeat these 2 rows until 50 stitches remain on needle. Cast off.
Work the ribbing for the front in the same way, but instead of 66 stitches you will pick up 78 stitches.
Using 3.00mm needles, pick up stitches across the top of each front shoulder, including the side of the neck ribbing (about 25 stitches). Work k 1, p 1 rib for 4 rows, then make three buttonholes evenly across the ribbing: rib 2, * cast off 4 stitches, rib 3, * repeat * to * twice more, rib to end.
Next row: rib 2, * cast on 4 stitches, rib 3, * repeat * to * twice more, rib to end.
Work 3 more rows of rib, then cast off.

### MAKE UP

Overlap the ribbed bands with the garter stitch band at the tops of the armholes and sew them together. Sew the tops of the sleeves into the armholes. Press work lightly on the wrong side with a warm iron over a slightly damp cloth. Sew up the side and sleeve seams and press. Sew buttons onto the garter-stitch band of the back shoulders to match the buttonholes.

## KNICKERS

### FRONT

Using 3.25mm needles, begin at top by casting on 70 stitches. Work 6 rows in k 1, p 1 rib, working into the backs of the stitches of the 1st row.
**Next row:** * Rib across 3 stitches, yrn, work 2 tog, rep from * to end of row.
Rib 9 rows straight.
Change to stocking stitch and work 6 rows straight. On next and every following 8th row, increase next to the edge stitch at both ends of the row until there are 86 stitches on needle. Work 7 rows straight. Cast off 3 stitches at beginning of each of next 18 rows (32 stitches). Cast off.

### BACK

Using 3.25mm needles, cast on 80 stitches. Work ribbing top in the same way as for front. Slip 24 stitches. Join wool to next stitch and k 32 stitches, turn.
**Next row:** P stitches of previous row and 4 stitches further along ribbing, turn.

**Next row:** K stitches of previous row and 4 stitches further, turn. Continue working backwards and forwards in stocking stitch, taking 4 stitches more each time until all stitches have been worked. Work 5 rows straight.
On next and every following 8th row increase next to the edge stitch at both ends of the row until there are 96 stitches on needle. Work 7 rows straight. Cast off 4 stitches at beginning of each of next 10 rows, then 3 stitches at beginning of each of next 8 rows (32 stitches). Cast off. Sew the two sets of 32 stitches between the legs together.

### LEG RIBBING

Holding right side of work towards you, and using 3.00mm needles, pick up and knit through every stitch along one leg edge. On the original there were 60 stitches. Work 2.5cm in k 1, p 1 rib. Cast off. Complete second leg in same way.

### TO MAKE UP

Press work on wrong and then on right side with a hot iron over a damp cloth. Sew up the side seams and press these. Thread the elastic in and out of the holes round the waist and join ends.

# Knitting guilds

Craftsmen's guilds of past centuries operated as highly professional and regulated unions, requiring rigorous training and standards for admission as a Master tradesman. Knitting guilds today are very different. They operate as membership-based organisations and welcome knitters of all skill levels, from beginners to experts.

Knitting guilds are inclusive, welcoming places for knitters to learn, access resources and feel a sense of community.

Knitting guilds or knitting associations exist today in countries all around the world. They focus on promoting the craft of knitting and educating members through sharing of information, skills and patterns. They are often run by volunteers and their activities are supported by membership subscriptions.

Australia has several state-based knitting guilds, which hold activities that include talks, presentations, classes, workshops, special events and retail opportunities. They hold regular knitting groups for those who enjoy practising their craft with like-minded people and high standards are encouraged through exhibiting of members' work. An important role for knitting guilds is to communicate with members, via regular newsletters, websites and social media.

Some guilds also have libraries of knitting books, patterns or equipment, or archives that help preserve examples of knitting from the past.

The Knitters' Guild NSW has nearly 800 members who belong to over 25 local Guild groups. The Handknitters Guild of South Australia also has local knitting groups across the state. The Handknitters Guild of Victoria is based in Melbourne and participates in knitting events across Victoria, such as a summer school, yarn and craft markets and craft shows. Some knitting guilds are linked to local community knitting groups or groups that knit for charity.

In addition to handknitting guilds, there are also organisations that promote machine knitting, such as the NSW Machine Knitters Association and, in the UK, The Guild for Machine Knitters.

# Noni

This pattern is another that plays to the Depression and postwar market for inexpensive clothing that looks like luxury. In this case, a regular wool yarn has been brushed with a steel brush to raise a nap that looks like mohair.

*Olive Ketels' Exclusive Knitwear for Young Folk*, No.2, 1947.

**Materials:** 250g Australian Alpaca Barn Panache 4 ply 80% alpaca, 20% merino wool in Baby Pink; small quantity of Panache yarn in Ecru; 1 pair each of 6.5mm and 3.75mm needles; wire brush; 1 metre of 12mm wide ribbon or tape.
**Measurements:** Length from top of shoulder, 28cm; length underarm, 14cm; sleeve underarm, 33cm; width around underarm, 71cm. As it is designed to be worn open at the front, this will fit a six- to eight-year old.

## BODY

The body of the bolero is knitted in one piece. With 6.5mm needles, cast on 107 stitches and knit seven rows in moss stitch.
**Next row:** Moss 7, k to last 7 stitches, moss 7.
**Next row:** Moss 7, purl to last 7 stitches, moss 7.
Repeat these 2 rows until work measures 14cm, then divide stitches for armholes as follows:

**Right front:**
**1st row:** Moss 7, k 21, Turn work
**2nd row:** Cast off 5, purl to last 7 stitches, moss 7.
**3rd row:** Moss 7, k to end.
**4th row:** P 2 tog, p to last 7 stitches, moss 7.
Keeping moss stitch border of 7 stitches, continue in stocking stitch until armhole measures 11.5cm. Knit 5 rows moss stitch. Cast off.
**Back:**
Take next 51 stitches.
**1st row:** Cast off 5, k to end.
**2nd row:** Cast off 5, p to end.
Knit 2 tog at beginning of next four rows, then continue in stocking stitch until armhole measures 11.5cm. Knit 5 rows moss stitch. Cast off.
**Left front:**
Take remaining 28 stitches.
**1st row:** Cast off 5, k to last 7 stitches, moss 7.

Paton's 'Bonny Sports' wool in blue was recommended for this garment. We chose an alpaca-wool blend which brushed up nicely for the faux-mohair look.

**2nd row:** Moss 7, p to end.
**3rd row:** K 2 tog, k to last 7 stitches, moss 7.
Keeping a moss stitch border of 7 stitches, knit in stocking stitch until armhole measures 11.5cm. Knit 5 rows in moss stitch. Cast off.

## SLEEVES

With 3.25mm needles, cast on 27 stitches and knit 10 rows in moss stitch.
**11th row:** K 4, k twice into every stitch to last 4 stitches, k 4 (46 stitches).
**12th row:** Purl.
Knit in stocking stitch until work measures 33cm.
Cast off 3 stitches at beginning of next two rows, then k 2 tog at beginning and end of every 4th row three times, then every 2nd row until 22 stitches remain.
**Next row:** P 2 tog, p to end.
Cast off 7 stitches at beginning of next two rows. Knit 11.5cm in moss stitch on remaining 7 stitches. Cast off.
Knit other sleeve to match.

## BOW

With white wool and 3.25mm needles, cast on 9 stitches, and knit in moss stitch for 36cm. Cast off.

## TO MAKE UP

With darning needle, finish off all ends securely. Press pieces flat. Sew up sleeve seams and insert sleeves, joining top of sleeve across front and back of bodice to form small yoke. Stitch ribbon or tape down front and around neck to keep garment in shape. Tie bow and applique firmly. Use the steel brush to brush garment, using a firm, steady stroke. Hold brush in palm of right hand, and with garment over left hand, brush away from you. This must be done carefully to gain a thick, even pile. After washing, run wire brush lightly over garment. This will bring pile up as new.

# Knitting for victory

The first half of the twentieth century in Australia saw a great deal of handknitting to meet the needs of soldiers fighting abroad in the First and Second World Wars.

During the First World War, Australia experienced a shortage of fabrics and ready-made clothing. Wool, however, was in plentiful supply and there was a massive movement knitting socks, scarves, balaclavas, vests and kneepads for soldiers on the frontline—a practical way that people at home could contribute to the war effort. A continuous supply of clean new socks was especially needed, as there was no way for the soldiers to wash or dry their clothing. The wet and muddy trenches in France caused woollen socks to rot, resulting in trench foot, a nasty condition in which feet swelled and rotted.

Thousands of men, women and children knitted more than 1.3 million pairs of socks, which were sent abroad, often with a personal note from the knitter. Jack Pickrell, a young soldier serving in France received several such notes, including one from eleven-year-old Joe Barlow who wrote, 'God Bless you soldier boy'.

Organisations such as the Australian Comforts Fund, the Soldiers' Sock Fund and the Australian Red Cross coordinated knitting groups and dispatched items to the troops. Every day in the Melbourne Town Hall, up to 40 women gathered to knit. On the banks of the Murray River in New South Wales, Corowa Public School's 'sock barometer' counted a grand total of 140 pairs knitted. In Sydney, the Soldiers' Sock Fund gave talks to knitters on how to make the perfect sock and published 'The Grey Sock' booklet with detailed knitting instructions. In her book *The Home Front*, Jan Bassett described Australia's knitting effort:

> *Soon after the war began, women and girls were knitting socks, scarves and*

LEFT Unsubtle advertisements such as this from 1941 were commonplace in the war years; ABOVE May Gibbs created this hand-coloured gumnut babies print in about 1915.

*balaclavas, for the soldiers. They knitted at home, on trams, in churches. When they ran out of knitting needles, they made new ones from bicycle spokes: when they ran out of dye, they used onion skins and wattle bark; when they ran out of wool, they learnt to spin their own.*

Unfortunately, not all of the socks that were knitted made it to the frontline. The war office had strict standards that had to be met, and many pairs of socks were rejected. Beginner knitters were advised to practice on facewashers, mufflers and mittens before tackling socks.

As war began again in November 1939, there was a call from the Second Australian Imperial Force and the Royal Australian Air Force for socks, sweaters and scarves. The Australian Government produced guidelines for the garments that could be knitted to support the troops in the harsh conditions they faced. Companies such as Melbourne's Patons & Baldwins produced booklets of patterns that met these guidelines. By the end of the Second World War, the Australian Comforts Fund alone had knitted more than 3 million pairs of socks, 1 million balaclavas, nearly 600,000 woollen gloves and 375,000 jumpers.

Knitting has also featured in Australian remembrance ceremonies. On Anzac Day in 2015, to commemorate the Gallipoli centenary, Melbourne's Federation Square was covered in handknitted and crocheted poppies to honour fallen soldiers. On Armistice Day in 2018, 60,000 knitted poppies blanketed the grounds of the Australian War Memorial to mark the centenary of the end of the First World War, with each poppy representing an Australian life lost.

# References

*5000 Poppies: A Community Tribute of Respect and Rememberance*, 5000poppies.wordpress.com

*About Wool...: Information about the Wool Industry from the Australian Wool Corporation*. Melbourne: Australian Wool Corporation, 1988–1989

Abrams, L., 'Ideals of Womanhood in Victorian Britain', *History Trails: Victorian Britain*, bbc.co.uk/history/trail/victorian_britain/women_home/ideals_womanhood_01.shtml

Alexander, J. (ed.), *Australian Yarn Art: Knitting Stories & Designs*. Melbourne: Crown Content, 2002. See 'Introduction'.

*Australian Dictionary of Biography*, adb.anu.edu.au

*Australian Home Journal and Patons' Knitting Topics*. Melbourne: Patons & Baldwins (Australia) Ltd., c.1930s

*Australian Textiles—The Early Days. Technology in Australia 1788–1988*, austehc.unimelb.edu.au/tia/272.html

Bassett, J., *The Home Front, 1914–1918*. Melbourne: Oxford University Press, 1983, cited in ergo.slv.vic.gov.au/explore-history/australia-wwi/home-wwi/homefront

Clave-Brule M., et al., 'Managing Anxiety in Eating Disorders with Knitting', *Eat Weight Disord.*, March 2009, 14(1):e1-5

Corkhill, B., et al., 'The Benefits of Knitting for Personal and Social Wellbeing in Adulthood: Findings from an International Survey', *British Journal of Occupational Therapy*, 2013, 76(2), 50–57

Corkhill, B., Stitchlinks and Davidson, C., Royal United Hospital, Bath, 'Exploring the Effects of Knitting on the Experience of Chronic Pain—A Qualitative Study', stitchlinks.com/pdfsNewSite/research/Poster%20Britsh%20Pain%20Society%20March%202009%20copy.pdf

Craft Yarn Council's 2014 Tracking Study, craftyarncouncil.com/know.html

Crawford, S., and Waller, J., *A Stitch in Time: Vintage Knitting Patterns, 1930–1959*, v.2, 2011

*Encyclopedia Britannica*, Britannica.com

Gardner, S., *A–Z of Knitting*. Malvern (SA): Country Bumpkin Publications, 2006. See 'The History of Knitting'.

Geda, Y., et al., 'Engaging in Cognitive Activities, Aging and Mild Cognitive Impairment: A Population-Based Study', *The Journal of Neuropsychiatry and Clinical Neurosciences*, 2011, 23(2): 149–154, doi:10.1176/appi.neuropsych.23.2.149. ncbi.nlm.nih.gov/pmc/articles/PMC3204924/

'Tweed Guide: The Curiously Compelling Story of Tweed', gentlemansgazette.com/tweed-guide-harris-history-styles-patterns

Green, S., 'The History of Knitting', *Creative Knitting*, Issue 10, Winter 2005

*Guinness World Records*, guinnessworldrecords.com

*Handknitters Guild*, handknittersguild.wordpress.com/about/

*History of Clothing*, historyofclothing.com

'History of Wool', bigmerino.com.au/history-of-wool

Hitches, B., *Wool in Australia 1788–1988*. Parkville (Vic.): Communications Department, Australian Wool Corporation, 1988

'Industrial Revolution', history.com/topics/industrial-revolution

*Knit One Give One*, kogo.org.au

*Knitters Guild of NSW*, knittersguildnsw.org.au

*Knitting and Crochet Guild (UK)*, kcguild.org.uk

*Knitting Nannas*, knitting-nannas.com/about.php

Lord, M., *Knitting Basics*. Sydney: Murdoch Books, 2012

McCreadie, M., 'The Evolution of Education in Australia', Internet Family History Association of Australia

*Machine Knitters Guild*, guild-mach-knit.org.uk/aboutus/histg.php

Macintyre, S., *A Concise History of Australia*. Port Melbourne (Vic.): Cambridge University Press, 2009, (3rd edition). See Chapter 8, 'Golden Age, 1946–1974'.

*Modern Developments in the Australian Woollen Industry*. Associated Enterprises of Yarra Falls Spinning Company Pty Ltd and Australian Knitting Mills Limited, c.1923

*Patons, Knitting Topics*. Melbourne: Patons & Baldwins (Australia) Ltd, c.1930s

*Pussy Hat Project*, pussyhatproject.com

*Red Cross Australia*, redcross.org.au

Rutt, R., *A History of Hand Knitting*. London (UK): Interweave Press, 1987

*Sheep Online*, sheeponline.com.au

Simpson, M., 'Industrial Revolution in Australia—Impact on the Wool Industry', maas.museum/inside-the-collection/2016/03/31/industrial-revolution-wool

*The Australian Women's Weekly*, from 1939 and 1941, trove.nla.gov.au/newspaper/title/112

*The Conversation*, theconversation.com

'The Industrial Revolution in Australia', sovereignhilledblog.com/2013/02/06/the-industrial-revolution-in-australia

*The Knitting Guild Association*, tkga.org/about-us

*Trove*, trove.nla.gov.au

*V is for Vintage*, visforvintage.net

Waller, J. (ed.), *A Stitch in Time: Knitting and Crochet Patterns of the 1920s, 1930s & 1940s*. London: Duckworth, 1972. Quote 'the great age of Hollywood' is on page 59.

'Making pouches for orphaned joeys', wires.org.au/wildlife-information/making-pouches-for-orphaned-joeys

*World Wide Knit in Public Day*, wwkipday.com

*Wrap with Love*, wrapwithlove.org/about-wrap-with-love

# List of Illustrations

The studio photographs in this book were taken by Craig Mackenzie, National Library of Australia.

**14** JAM Project, *Yarnbombing the Lower Ground Dining Area of Central Park Mall*, 2016, www.flickr.com/photos/jam_project/27162716361, reproduced under CC BY-SA 2.0: creativecommons.org/licenses/by-sa/2.0/; **15** JAM Project, *Queen Babs Yarnbombing Workshop at Work-Shop in Redfern*, 2016, www.flickr.com/photos/jam_project/26051512223/, reproduced under CC BY-SA 2.0: creativecommons.org/licenses/by-sa/2.0/; **20** 'March of the Mode by Rene', page 6 in *The Australian Women's Weekly*, 27 February 1937, trove.nla.gov.au/newspaper/page/4616184; **23** S.T. Gill, *November*, c.1842, nla.cat-vn1980207; **27** 'Charm in Every Trim Chic Line', page 10 in *The Australian Women's Weekly*, 27 February 1937, trove.nla.gov.au/newspaper/page/4627066; **29 (upper)** JAM Project, *Yarnbombing Ward Park for the 2016 Surry Hills Festival*, 2016, www.flickr.com/photos/jam_project/29414958033, reproduced under CC BY-SA 2.0: creativecommons.org/licenses/by-sa/2.0/; **29 (lower)** JAM Project, *International Yarnbombing Day 2016 at Redfern Park*, 2016, www.flickr.com/photos/jam_project/27036865554/, reproduced under CC BY-SA 2.0: creativecommons.org/licenses/by-sa/2.0/; **32** 'Created in Hollywood ... Youthful Cardigan', page 22 in *The Australian Women's Weekly*, 16 August 1941, trove.nla.gov.au/newspaper/article/51942881; **36** 'It Plays the Game', page 7 in *The Australian Women's Weekly*, 25 March 1939, trove.nla.gov.au/newspaper/article/51270952; **41** 'With the Hall Mark of Paris', page 20 in *The Australian Women's Weekly*, 25 March 1939, trove.nla.gov.au/newspaper/article/51270946; **43** Cover of *The Australian Women's Weekly*, 6 May 1944, trove.nla.gov.au/newspaper/page/4726086; **46** 'Knitted Argyle Is New U.S. Fashion', page 53 in *The Australian Women's Weekly*, 1 April 1953, trove.nla.gov.au/newspaper/article/40465747; **50** 'Engaging New Anny Blatt Model', page 9 in *The Australian Women's Weekly*, 25 March 1939, trove.nla.gov.au/newspaper/article/51270954; **53** Wolfgang Sievers, *Winding Wool at Yarra Falls Limited, Abbotsford, Victoria*, 1960, nla.cat-vn4397003; **56** 'Special Knitting Pattern: The Checked Coat', page 6 in *The Argus* (Melbourne), 7 May 1936, trove.nla.gov.au/newspaper/article/11032933; **59** 'Hand-made Knitteds to Win Your Heart', page 3 in *The Australian Women's Weekly*, 25 March 1939, trove.nla.gov.au/newspaper/page/4627012; **62** 'An Aristocrat in White and Scarlet', page 47 in *The Australian Women's Weekly*, 13 April 1935, trove.nla.gov.au/newspaper/article/47231523; **64** Wolfgang Sievers, *Bruck Mills, Wangaratta, Victoria*, 1950, nla.cat-vn2641864; **65** UntitledImages, *Owner Helping Employees and Being Collaborative*, 2017, iStock image 865612542; **71** 'This Week's Knitting Pattern: Pyramid Pullover', page 7 in *Sunday Mail* (Brisbane), 27 July 1952, trove.nla.gov.au/newspaper/page/10330660; **75 (lower)** 'Just the Thing for Sports', page 2 in *The Australian Women's Weekly*, 25 March 1939, trove.nla.gov.au/newspaper/page/4627058; **76** Jacob Lund, *Hands of Senior Men Holding Knitting Needles and Wool Yarn*, Shutterstock image 1296208306; **77 (left)** V_Sot_Visual_Content, *Beige Knitwear Fabric Texture with Pigtails*, Shutterstock image 1572720457; **77 (right)** Sarah Johnston Chinnery, *Man Carrying Two Fishing Rods and Two Bait Tins Walking up a Boat Ramp, Sandringham, Victoria*, c.1955, nla.cat-vn4554392; **81** 'Of Course, Men Like Smart Knitteds', page 58 in *The Australian Women's Weekly*, 25 April 1936, trove.nla.gov.

au/newspaper/article/46463667; **82** Robin Smith, *Bales of Fine Merino Wool on Sale at an Auction, Sydney*, c.2009, nla.cat-vn8067347; **83** Frank Hurley, *Merino Ram Close up*, between 1910 and 1962, nla.cat-vn118907; **86** 'Smart and Snug-fitting: Man's Pullover', page 3 in *The Australian Women's Weekly*, 15 June 1940, trove.nla.gov.au/newspaper/article/47484427; **90** 'Designed for the Sportsman', page 55 in *The Australian Women's Weekly*, 4 August 1954, trove.nla.gov.au/newspaper/article/51192885; **91** Liam Driver, *Shearer Trevor Pike Works on a Sheep for His Team The Spinning Knitwits as They Compete in the Back to Back Wool Challenge at Tocal Homestead in the Hunter Valley*, 2008, Liam Driver/Newspix; **97** *Red Cross Trauma Teddies*, courtesy Australian Red Cross; **100** 'Angora Wool Trims this Little Girl's Pull-over' page 33 in *Country Life Knitting Book*, 1940s, nla.cat-vn3304207; **105** 'Charming Frock for Little Girl', page 22 in *The Australian Women's Weekly*, 8 May 1937, trove.nla.gov.au/newspaper/article/52244728; **107** Guy Arnoux, *Je ne saurais trop louer les citoyennnes patriotes qui ont fourni les soldats de tout ce qui manque aux magasins de la Nation*, 1918, nla.cat-vn7765679; **111** 'Paired off in Wool', page 33 in *Australian Home Journal*, 1 April 1950, nla.cat-vn1427091; **114** 'Child's Bolero with Rose Trimming in Fair Isle', page 15 in in *Australian Home Journal*, 2 May 1949, nla.cat-vn1427091; **118** 'Fredrick', pages 11 in *Olive Ketels' Exclusive Knitwear for Young Folk*, 1947, nla.cat-vn413889; **121** H.K. Browne, 'The Wine Shop', opposite page 109 in *A Tale of Two Cities* by Charles Dickens, 1859, nla.cat-vn2294059; **125** 'Cardigan 2–4 Years', between pages 16 and 17 in *What Children Wear in Knitting & Crochet* by Ella Allan, 1930–1931, nla.cat-vn2099081; **134** 'Douglas: Twin Sets Are Ideal for Two-year-olds' page 4 in *Olive Ketels' Exclusive Knitwear for Young Folk*, 1947, nla.cat-vn413889; **137 (upper)** David Jackson, *Earliest Knitted Items in the Victoria & Albert's Collection, Made in 300–499 AD, Excavated in Egypt*, commons.wikimedia.org/wiki/File:BLW_Pair_of_socks.jpg, reproduced under CC BY-SA 2.0: creativecommons.org/licenses/by-sa/2.0/uk/deed.en; **137 (lower)** Master Bertram, *The Buxtehude Altar, Visit of the Angel*, c.1405, commons.wikimedia.org/wiki/File:KnittingMadonna.jpg; **142** JAM Project, *Knit the Campus Workshop at Optus Headquarters in Macquarie Park*, 2016, www.flickr.com/photos/jam_project/28666404814/, reproduced under CC BY-SA 2.0: creativecommons.org/licenses/by-sa/2.0/; **147** 'Noni', page 45 in *Olive Ketels' Exclusive Knitwear for Young Folk*, 1947, nla.cat-vn413889; **148** *Is Your Man One of the Lucky Ones, Lux* book supplement, 1941, nla.cat-vn6894974; **149** May Gibbs, *Sister Susie's Sewing Shirts for Soldiers*, c.1915, nla.cat-vn620155.

## Acknowledgements

The idea for this book has its origins in Trove, the National Library of Australia's content aggregator, which is a rich resource for vintage knitting patterns. The models in this book are Library staff members and the children of Library staff members. Much of the content in this book comes from the wider Library community and our dedicated volunteers.

The Library would like to thank Judith Robertson for retyping the patterns; Lesley Paton and Carolyn Tow for researching and writing additional material; Anne Lewis for assistance with pattern proofreading; and Lynda Carmody, Aaron Minehan, April Hoffman, Minnie Craft and Rupert Sheppard for modelling the garments. The Library would especially like to thank the following Library staff members and volunteers who knitted garments for this book:

| | |
|---|---|
| Anne Lewis | *Dorothea* (p48) |
| Anne O'Hara | *Jack* (p69) |
| Antoinette Buchanan | *Fredrick* (p119); *Josephine* (p124) |
| Beverly Burne | *Douglas* (p132) |
| Cynthia Wallace | *Vivian* (p33) |
| Eleanor Hing Fay | *Lynette* (p96) |
| Elizabeth Davey | *Beverly* (p111) |
| Jennifer Phillips | *Robert* (p91) |
| Jenny Harber | *Barbara* (p43) |
| Judith Robertson | *Pamela* (p101) |
| Kate Boesen | *Florence* (p36) |
| Kerrie Spinks | *Noni* (p146) |
| Laura Iseman | *William* (p84) |
| Lynda Carmody | *Helen* (p60) |
| Lynne Johnson | *Stuart* (p79) |
| Margaret Mitchell | *Clyde* (p72); *Jennifer* (p114) |
| Mary Bowron | *Lorraine* (p104) |
| Melody Lord | *Margaret* (p54) |
| Ros Hirst | *Lynette* (p96) |
| Samantha Edmonds | *Sandra* (p28) |
| Sarah Boulter | *Patricia* (p23) |
| Susan Frost | *David* (p129) |
| Tril Tyler | *Ian* (p141) |
| Vikki Clingan | *Judith* (p16) |

Published by National Library of Australia Publishing
Canberra ACT 2600

ISBN: 9781922507495




The National Library of Australia acknowledges Australia's First Nations Peoples—the First Australians—as the Traditional Owners and Custodians of this land and gives respect to the Elders—past and present—and through them to all Australian Aboriginal and Torres Strait Islander people.




Managing editor: Melody Lord
Designer: Astred Hicks, Design Cherry

Printed in China by RR Donnelley on FSC®-certified paper.

Find out more about NLA Publishing at nla.gov.au/stories/national-library-publishing.

A catalogue record for this book is available from the National Library of Australia